BEHIND
THE VEIL

★ ★ ★ ★ ★

A STAND AGAINST
GOVERNOR TIM WALZ

PAUL GAZELKA

★　★　★　★　★

BEHIND THE VEIL

★　★　★　★　★

A STAND AGAINST
GOVERNOR TIM WALZ

BEHIND THE VEIL by Paul Gazelka
Published by Perissos Publishers
Copyright 2024 by Paul Gazelka. All rights reserved.

ISBN: 979-8-9915080-0-1
Ebook ISBN: 979-8-9915080-1-8

I would like to dedicate this book to my wife, Maralee, who stood with me during many challenging days while I served as Minnesota's Senate majority leader. I would also like to dedicate this book to the amazing group of Minnesota senators and staff whom I served with at the Minnesota Capitol. Together we lowered the tone and made Minnesota a better place.

CONTENTS

BACKGROUND: BEHIND THE VEIL WITH GOVERNOR TIM WALZ

INTRODUCTION

I T'S BEEN MORE than twenty years since I wrote the book *Mar-ketplace Ministers*. I never imagined that since that time, I would run for public office and eventually end up being the Minnesota Senate majority leader. I had the privilege of serving and guiding a group of amazing Republican senators with a one-vote majority. We did this in a state, Minnesota, that was often completely controlled by Democrats.

Among many moments, I had the responsibility of governing *with* and *against* Governor Tim Walz during the COVID-19 pandemic, the riots spawned by the tragic death of George Floyd in Minneapolis, the growing crime and anti-police movement that followed, and the presidency of Donald Trump.

CHAPTERS RELATED TO GOVERNOR TIM WALZ BEGIN WITH CHAPTER 10

If you are looking for the chapters about my experiences with Governor Tim Walz, they begin with chapter 10. But I hope you read the stories throughout the book about how government can work better by people respecting and honoring each other, even in politics, and even when we disagree passionately.

I talk about political conversations I had with Governor Walz to capture the behind-the-veil discussions during the early months of the COVID-19 crisis and the Minneapolis riots after the death of

George Floyd. It was a tense time, and the conversations reflected how Tim Walz responds to pressure and use of emergency powers.

PEOPLE ARE ANGRY WITH EACH OTHER

People are angry, and that by itself accomplishes nothing good. James 1:20 says that "the anger of man does not achieve the righteousness of God" (NASB1995).

This book addresses the tone of American politics and offers a different way to lead. The principles I write about work for anyone, but my actions were a result of my distinctively Christian worldview.

Simple principles like treating people the way I want to be treated, doing good, loving mercy, being humble, and speaking the truth in love work for anyone who applies these timeless ideals.

Following these principles in politics did not mean I was weak, as some thought. But rather, it was a conscious choice not to govern by the "eye for an eye" way of political life. I always tried diplomacy first, and political war, if necessary, was last.

Sometimes political war is necessary, but that path should be carefully assessed first. Abraham Lincoln had no desire for war or a division in the union. But he reluctantly entered into war against the Confederates states, and once he was in, he was all in. Even so, when it was all over, he sought reconciliation with the defeated Southern states.

As I write this book in the summer of 2024, I see a huge need for more civility in our country. I understand that in a difficult world full of power-hungry dictators, we have to be tough. Our enemies around the world don't care if we are kind; they measure whether we are strong or weak.

I know it's important to stand up for our values and way of life when some have a much different agenda. But do we have to be rude and immovable with our fellow Americans?

In 2017 I attended a political event in Washington, DC. Part of the discussion focused on the growing divide between Republican and Democrat legislators in the House. According to the notes I took from the figures shared, 344 of the 435 legislators were ideologically similar in 1982. But in each election thereafter the similarities decreased so that by 2013 only four legislators shared similar ideologies with legislators across the political aisle. I wonder what it is like now.

Not having some legislators working in the middle to bridge the divide between the parties is a recipe for failure, gridlock, or worse. That does not mean folks agreeing to compromises with the other side are evil; they are just trying to make government work for conservatives, liberals, and everyone in between.

Today we are even more divided, and I see a lot more weakness and decay in our country than even ten years ago. United we stand; divided we fall. Part of that unity begins with being a lot more civil toward each other as fellow Americans. Civility begins by choosing to love one another, especially those that are different from us. It doesn't mean we remain quiet when we disagree. I'm diplomatically firm with my adversaries, but I'm still kind.

AMERICA IS PRECIOUS

It's up to us, like each generation before us, to do everything in our power to protect this more perfect union. I've traveled to enough countries to know there is no place like America. It's no wonder that people from every part of the world flock to America for a better life than where they came from. On the other hand, not many people leave our shores. That should be a clue that what we have in America is precious.

In America we may have passed the point of no return, where every action between the two sides brings even more division. If agreement and compromise are no longer sought out, we are all in deep trouble. The country must work for everyone so we have a voice.

What would politics look like according to the kingdom of God? How would a Christ-follower, like me, govern differently if given the chance? Would it look different at all?

There are certainly examples that I looked to in the Scriptures.

Daniel in the Old Testament had significant influence in a culture very different than his own. He valued King Darius, and when rivals tried to destroy him—actually kill him—through false accusations, to the relief of the king, Daniel prevailed. (See Daniel 6.)

David was a warrior king who was the fierce leader of his country. He wasn't afraid to fight for what was best for his country, and he was still a man after God's own heart (Acts 13:22).

Joseph was betrayed by his brothers and sold as a slave. But he rose to power in Egypt through the wisdom God placed in him. He ended up saving his own extended family and the Egyptian nation from a seven-year drought that would have led to mass starvation (Gen. 37, 39–45).

Men and women of faith clearly can be authentically who they are and make a meaningful difference in the political realm, regardless of what the state of affairs is.

I became the leader of Minnesota's Senate in 2017. I didn't realize it when I became the Senate leader, but stepping into political leadership requires sacrifice, enduring pain, and being misunderstood.

Even friends and family can believe some things that are not true. That happened to Jesus, with His own brothers not believing in Him. It also happened to David with his brothers and son. It happened to Joseph with his brothers.

But Jesus came in a different spirit; He loved all people. He was a friend to those who were outcasts in His time. Because of His example, I am compelled to try to do the same.

Democrats are not my enemy. That does not mean I agree with many of their positions, but I recognize their value as part of America and, more importantly, as people created in the image of God. Both sides can respond in inappropriate ways, but I choose to overcome evil with good and not respond with evil for evil.

After the death of George Floyd, I built new relationships with some black and Latino leaders in Minneapolis, like Pastor Jerry McAfee and Pastor Victor Martinez. I learned much more about the plight of those they represented by having continued conversations with them. I also built friendships with some from the indigenous community, including new friends like Todd Finney of the Oglala Lakota and Wahpekute Dakota people. I represented a central Minnesota region as a state senator, but as majority leader I represented the entire state.

Becoming the leader did not happen overnight for me. I had developed leadership skills in my private life, running my business, taking volunteer leadership roles, being promoted in a large corporation, and raising a family. Then I served in the House and the Senate for eight years. Even when I became the majority leader, I was still learning. There are not many mentors for this position. The higher you go in leadership, the less likely there is a how-to manual about how to do it. I was only the twenty-ninth leader of the Minnesota Senate in over 150 years.

I had to learn by simply doing it. I didn't watch a thirty-minute video and think I was the expert; that's for the armchair quarterbacks.

CONFRONTING GOVERNOR WALZ

When the COVID pandemic hit, along with the riots after the death of George Floyd, I found out that I excelled in a crisis; the bigger the crisis, the better I felt I was. Under intense pressure, my cool personality went to warm, but I never boiled over or flipped my lid. It was during this time that I had to confront Governor Walz about poor decisions he was making during that crisis season.

I was surrounded by an amazing team of Republican leaders. I generally acted more like a secretary of state, which meant I needed others around me, such as Mike Campbell and Senators Andrew Mathews and Mark Koran, to be more like a secretary of war.

WALZ IS THE VICE-PRESIDENTIAL CANDIDATE

I never dreamed that as I was finishing this book, Governor Walz would be selected as the running mate for presidential candidate Kamala Harris. It made the chapters related to Tim Walz's leadership mistakes even more important. I tried my best to be direct and honest about my assessment, even though it is mostly negative.

Finally, because the portion about Governor Tim Walz has national significance, I decided to discuss conversations between the governor and me that took place during the early COVID months and the Minneapolis riots after George Floyd's death. It reflects and verifies my presentation of the facts of that time. This is included in the last chapter.

In my time as leader I learned to live with a political target on my back. Democrats had all kinds of advocates pointing out my flaws or making them up if they needed to. But, surprisingly to me, there were also adversaries on my own side of the aisle, like Action 4 Liberty (A4L), Minnesota Gun Rights, and some ambitious Republicans.

I had to learn to navigate the minefields of politics. I had to accept the fact that people would give me nicknames, some of which I liked: Obi-Wan, Velvet Hammer, Peace Maker, Bulwark, Last Hope Against Democrat Domination, and Adult in the Room. And others gave me names I didn't like: RINO, Walz's girlfriend, Mr. Rogers, part of the establishment, part of the uniparty, and being accused of being the murderer of Senator Jerry Relph, who died of COVID-19.

After I stepped down as leader, Democratic Senator Nick Frentz said they weren't sure what it was going to be like after PGE. I asked what PGE was. He said it meant the Paul Gazelka era.

That is what this book is about—my time as leader and the things I experienced. My hope is that in some way this story stirs you to be involved, be informed, and make a difference in the realm of politics.

CHAPTER 1

I WASN'T LOOKING FOR POLITICS; POLITICS FOUND ME

I HAD BEEN A business owner my entire adult life. I was also very active in Christian ministry and wrote a book, *Marketplace Ministers*, about integrating my personal faith into daily living. The book was published in 2003, and at that time, I was traveling around the world, talking about the message of the book.

I believe God governs the affairs of nations and individuals, so as I share some of my stories in the political realm, I can't help but point out that God was at work, and I was simply along for the ride. In 2004 the road to politics was about to open up to me, but I was not looking for it.

In the second half of 2003 I traveled to Australia to speak about ministry in the workplace. On one of the legs of the journey, to Sydney, I happened to sit on the plane next to Bill Hamon, a minister I had not met before. We were going to speak at the same conference. I shared about my book, and he was immediately intrigued because he was writing about the same topic. As we talked, he shared that he had a strong impression that I would have influence like Joseph and Daniel had in the Bible. As he spoke, I assumed his thoughts were about my growing role in the church, but both of those Old Testament figures had key governmental roles.

A few months later I was ministering at a conference in Denver with Dave Duell. After the conference I was invited over to his house for a scrumptious meal. As we talked, he shared that he had a strong impression that I was going to be a mayor or something like that. Again, I assumed the impression was related to church government, not political government.

A month or so after that happened, I was at a Christian conference in Minneapolis. As I walked into the event, a young lady came up to me and said, "You carry yourself like Tim Pawlenty." Pawlenty was Minnesota's governor, and at that point, I had never met him. Again, it seemed odd.

Finally, within another month, I was sitting in my local church, and my pastor stopped his message. He looked at me and said he saw a governmental mantle all over me.

I had four unique impressions from four different people within six months, all pointing me toward government. Even then I still thought it was church government.

I bring this up because I have found that God often speaks through other people to help us get where we need to go. God was preparing my heart for a significant change of course in my life, and He was underlining it for me.

REPRESENTATIVE DALE WALZ ASKS ME TO RUN FOR HOUSE

Shortly after these encounters, the Minnesota state representative for my area, Dale Walz, called me and asked if we could meet. I had never met Representative Walz, but I felt honored that he wanted to meet me.

I asked him to come by my insurance office, and when he arrived, we went back to my private conference room. As we chatted, he finally got around to the real reason he wanted to visit with me. He wanted me to run for his seat in the Minnesota House. He shared with me that he had been diagnosed with Parkinson's disease and he needed to retire from the House. He asked if I would run in his place.

Wow, that was a bombshell. I certainly wasn't expecting that. I really wasn't involved in politics. I cared deeply about many issues, but I never had thought about the idea of running for public office. Suddenly the opportunity presented itself to me. This was no easy decision for me. I easily could have said no. I was very active in my business, and I was involved in ministry. Even more importantly, Maralee and I still had our five children at home.

But I was intrigued with the idea, and the four unusual impressions from ministry-oriented people made it more curious. No was not the answer, but was yes the answer? I talked to my wife and some of my mentors and family, and all of them thought I should do it—except my mom. She rightly said, "What about your family?" How could I take care of my family back at home two and a half hours from the Capitol, still run my insurance agency, and be a state representative?

As Maralee and I pondered this dilemma, we both thought I should do it, but we needed a way for it to work for the family too. We decided that if I were elected as a state representative, we would move to the Twin Cities as a family every year for the session. Each session lasts for about five months, from January to May. We didn't have all the details yet, like what to do about our children's education and where we would live, but it seemed like it would work.

When I shared the idea with my mom, the lone thumbs down, she also gave me the green light. I didn't need her approval, but it was nice to have everyone on board with this major decision. I felt called to politics. It wasn't just going to be another job; it felt more important than that.

Not long after that, Maralee and I were vacationing in Bradenton, Florida, and ran into a stranger. His daughter lived in Brainerd, Minnesota, with her husband, Brian Lehman. That's where we lived. A few days later we got back to Brainerd and went to get lunch at a local taco place. As we were standing in line, I turned to the person behind me, introduced myself to him, and then asked who he was. "I'm Brian Lehman," he said.

I then shared with him that I had just met his father-in-law in Florida a few days earlier. As we talked, I found out that he graduated from Oral Roberts University, as I had. He also ran for the House but in Oklahoma. And the short story is, he became my campaign manager, along with Sue Hilgart.

I knew nothing about how to run a campaign, but Brian Lehman, a local business consultant and prior Oklahoma House candidate, showed me the ropes.

CAMPAIGNING FOR THE HOUSE SEAT

I began campaigning immediately. First I needed to be endorsed by local Republicans. I personally called hundreds of delegates to ask for their support. I was being challenged by the local BPOU (basic political organizational unit) chair, or more accurately, I was challenging her. That win happened quickly. Then I began the work of convincing my local community that they would be best served if I were their local representative.

We built a team of supporters and began the hard work of knocking on every residential door, asking for support. We put up over five hundred campaign signs in yards of anyone who said we could. I attended local community events, like art in the park, church picnics, local civic group luncheons, the county fair, parades, etc. If I was made aware of a local event, I was there to meet the people. Campaigning is a full-time job.

If you are interested in politics, campaigns are a good place to get your feet wet. While working alongside a candidate you believe in, you get to learn the ropes about what it takes to win. I had a few volunteers that eventually went on to run for elected office, like Representative Josh Heintzeman and Mayors Brian Lehman and Angel Zierden. Other volunteers ended up taking prominent roles for elected officials, like Mandy Heffron, who works for Congresswoman Michelle Fischbach. Campaigning also opens unique doors to meet some very interesting people.

PRESIDENT GEORGE W. BUSH VISITS ST. CLOUD, MINNESOTA— GOD SAVED US SEATS

President George W. Bush was slated to speak in St. Cloud, Minnesota, and we were given VIP seats at the event. Maralee, one of our children, and I were given tickets to the bleachers behind the podium. They told us to come two hours early to get the seats. Unfortunately we only were there about an hour ahead of time. I hate being late, and I knew that we were likely not going to get good seats, if we got any at all.

As I assumed, the people were already packed like sardines in the bleachers. It appeared that there were no seats left. After I stood there for a few minutes, I saw what appeared to be three seats, right in the middle, at the same level as the platform. I thought that they must be saving them for someone. After a few minutes more, I decided to make everyone stand up so we could get to the middle of the bleachers and ask if the seats were available. We plowed through the crowd, inching our way past the folks standing up to let us by. We finally got to the three open seats and asked those sitting there if the seats next to them were available. Sure enough, nobody was saving them. It honestly felt like God had saved them just for us.

We were positioned about fifteen feet behind the president. I was positioned off the president's left shoulder, but on national TV it looked like I was standing right next to him. Friends from other states called me after the event to let me know they saw me standing with the president. We felt special.

Maralee was directly behind the president, and only her hair was visible on television. She is a praying woman, and she knew her assignment was to pray for the president while he spoke. I think God is always beckoning His followers to pray for their leaders, regardless of party affiliation, and this was a perfect opportunity for Maralee to do so. Later we found out that a friend of ours, Cathy Jo, was directly in front of the president, praying for him as well.

BRIEF MEETING WITH PRESIDENT GEORGE W. BUSH

After we got back from the event with President Bush, I was quick to tell all my friends that I had a brief meeting with the president of the United States, which actually meant that I shook his hand as he went by.

The campaign for the House seat was a lot more work than I expected, but I put all my energy into it. I did not know that it was a swing district and that my challenger, Senator Don Samuelson, was predicted to win. After a long career in the state senate, he had been defeated two years earlier but won my side of the Senate district. He didn't want to give up his role in politics yet and thought he would be elected to the House.

In that first election, the entire family was helping on the campaign. At parades we would try to put a "Gazelka for House" sticker on everyone. Then we would march through the parade route. I would jog-walk the parade route, shaking the hands of as many parade goers as I could. Maralee was often by my side, doing the same thing. The rest of the family would hand out candy and more stickers.

VOTE FOR MY DAD!

At the time, our youngest daughter was three. The Brainerd parade had at least ten thousand folks watching from the sidewalks. Some crowds were five rows deep. As we approached the announcer's booth, where they tell the parade goers who is marching by, our daughter decided to put a sticker over her mouth. The announcer said, "Gazelka has stickered everything, even his daughter's mouth."

Our tiny three-year-old motioned for the microphone. As they put it near her mouth, she took the sticker off and shouted, "Vote for my dad!" The crowd roared! I could not have planned that any better.

Campaigning every day, meeting new people, and getting in front of large crowds was hard to get used to. As I got into the routine, it became a little easier, but I can't say I ever loved it. My kids were enthusiastic at first about campaigning for me, but over time, most of them preferred not to do it. I never demanded they help. I signed up for this role, but they did not. Some of my kids are more introverted, so being in front of large groups of people took a lot of effort on their part.

Maralee is also more introverted. She put all her energy into campaigning with me, and for her, as an introvert, that was a big sacrifice. We both felt called to this, but that didn't mean that every day was easy. But we had put our hand to the plow, and we were not going to quit. We planned to win.

When an election is winnable, each side hires staff to help the candidate to win. If the race is not close, independent money, apart from the candidate's, is not spent, and you definitely won't get a paid staffer for your campaign. If you are the one running for a government position, whether you get outside help is a pretty good indicator of if you have a chance to win.

As we came down to the finish line and had the final debates, the lit pieces, or literature sent in the mail, got more aggressive on both sides. That also meant that it was a close race. If the race is not close, the campaign ads are sparse and not caustic.

GUY AND TERRY ST. MARTIN

As the race was nearing the end, we attended our local church, as was our weekly custom. We met a new couple on vacation from the Twin Cities who had decided to take in a service at our church. We connected with them easily and quickly built rapport. Their names were Guy and Terry St. Martin, and they lived in Brooklyn Park.

We had already been contemplating where we would live and where our kids would go to school if we won. We decided that if we won, our kids would go to school at Maranatha Christian Academy in Brooklyn Park. Guy and Terry had children about the same age as our kids that were already going to that school .

We wondered if the chance meeting with the St. Martins was set up by the Lord; later we knew it was.

FIRST ELECTION WIN

In November of 2004 I won my race to be the representative to the Minnesota House from our area. I was going to be a Minnesota legislator. I really had no idea what it was going to be like. I had tons of zeal but very little understanding about what it takes to govern. My friend Congressman Tom Emmer also won a seat in the Minnesota House, and that was his beginning as well. Minnesota Speaker of the House Melissa Hortman was also in that class.

In the Minnesota House, Republicans are on the right side of the chamber and Democrats are on the left side. I was assigned to the area affectionally called the dog pound by Republican House members. Part of that area, the very back, was coveted by GOP legislators because it could not be viewed from the gallery above. Senior members picked this area for their floor desks. If they were bored during a long floor debate, they could watch a movie on their laptops, and no one would be the wiser.

I sat right next to Greg Blaine, the House member from the southern half of our shared Senate district. He was assigned to get me up to speed. Greg was a dairy farmer and somehow found a way to keep his cows milked daily while also serving as a House member.

Most rural members have an extra challenge of trying to balance their personal responsibilities with the responsibilities of being a legislator. That's part of the reason rural legislators get a stipend to cover the cost of housing expenses for an apartment next to the Capitol. Even so, trying to live in two separate places is never easy.

Maralee and I chose to move our entire family to the Twin Cities during the session. The House provided six months of housing rental reimbursement up to a set amount. At first I started to look for an apartment next to the Capitol that we could rent for six months and pack our whole family into. What was I thinking?

Maralee put her foot down. She said that if we were going to live in the Twin Cites as a family, we needed a nice house near where our kids were going to school, and she wanted to live near the St. Martins. Maralee moved into action and called Terry to ask her for help. Sure enough, Terry found a house for us to rent just a few doors down from their home. It was a perfect fit.

Terry and Guy were important new friends in a new community. They had our backs. When a couple of our children struggled as teenagers, Terry and Guy were important confidants. We laughed and cried together over some of the challenges all of us were experiencing raising teenagers.

So while I was getting ready to become a lawmaker, God was helping us tuck our kids into a good spot. That gave Maralee and me great comfort, knowing that this calling did not have to mean that our kids were forgotten.

DOC SEVERSON

I met my first important ally, Representative Dan "Doc" Severson on the first day in office. He came up to me and told me he "prayed me into office." He was looking for more like-minded Christian social conservatives, like me, to serve alongside him. We became instant friends. Doc had served our nation in a career as a Top Gun Navy fighter pilot. Now he was putting those leadership skills to good use as a legislator.

I had no experience as a legislator, as my background was business and ministry. It took me a while to get up to speed. I understood the issues, but converting that knowledge to bills and the process took some time.

I was assigned a legislative assistant, Jason Fossum, who had served the prior representative from our area. He helped me understand the process of writing a bill and getting it through the House. When I would say something that didn't work in the political arena, he would give me background on why. Many years later I had the opportunity to hire him for a key role in the Senate GOP.

The House is the louder and feistier of the two legislative chambers. I'm typically not loud and demonstrative, so as I got up to speed, I usually stayed quiet during that first two-year term.

I built legislative relationships on both sides of the aisle and honed my views on legislative issues. As a citizen, issues were clear cut, but as a legislator, I found that some issues are not as clear cut as a sound bite. Legislators pass legislation, but if everything were clear cut, we would not need the courts to sort out whether people are violating the laws we passed. Each legislative decision created a host of consequences, and if we were not careful with the exact wording, we created unintended consequences. It really was a learning experience.

The legislative session was a real pressure cooker. Republicans had the majority in the House, led by Speaker Steve Sviggum. Governor Tim Pawlenty was also a Republican. However, the Senate, like it had been for the last generation, was controlled by Democrats. That meant gridlock.

Speaker Sviggum had the impossible task of getting our rambunctious group, or caucus, to agree to a compromise with the Democrat-controlled Senate. Often Governor Pawlenty would have to intervene to break the log jam.

Compromise Is Required

Compromise is required in divided government, but it is never easy. When I was looking at the legislative process from the outside, I never really understood how difficult it was, and when compromise happened, I assumed the legislators caved in to the other side. The truth was each side had to cave in to the other side. Neither side would get everything they wanted, and both sides would get some things they didn't want. That's the legislative process. Some say the process is like making sausage—it's very messy.

INCREMENTAL CHANGE

Minnesota is a purple state, and that means that often power will be shared by both parties. Change will often be incremental when activists on both sides want it all now.

William Wilberforce started as a member of England's Parliament in 1780. For decades he fought the scourge of slavery, and gradually, over time, he was instrumental in abolishing the slave trade in 1807, leading to the eventual abolishment of slavery in the United Kingdom in 1834. The process took over fifty years.[1]

After the Civil War in America ended, President Lincoln was willing to accept some provisions that did not give black people complete equality because he knew that the country would need to take steps to get to that grand and necessary goal of true equality for all.[2]

Booker T. Washington, a former slave, was a strong proponent of education in the black community right after the end of the Civil War. Though he wanted complete equality for our black brothers and sisters, he advocated for separate but equal policies while the country began to adjust to the end of slavery. He knew the Southern white leaders around him in Mississippi would squelch his ultimate goal if he went too fast.[3]

Important changes often take time. We should not be discouraged when we make incremental progress, gradually leading our state or country in the right direction. For change to be durable, you must reach the hearts of the people first. Legislation can be changed, but it can easily enough be changed back when the opposing side is in power—unless the people are with you.

PRO-LIFE LEGISLATION ADVANCES IN MINNESOTA

I was impressed with Governor Tim Pawlenty when I first took office, and even more so when I became leader of the Senate. He never had a GOP trifecta but managed to accomplish much for the pro-life movement through incremental change. Though the

Democratic majority in the Senate opposed his plans, Pawlenty was responsible for enacting the Positive Alternatives Act (HF952) in 2006. It was legislation that provided financial resources to organizations helping pregnant women bring their babies to term. He also helped guide 2006 legislation, HF4153, that required parental notification before performing an abortion on a minor. Pawlenty guided these incremental changes with wit and grace. I was glad I had the privilege to co-author these measures as a House member.

As a side note, when Democrats took complete control of Minnesota's House, Senate, and governorship in 2022, all pro-life advances were lost.

Meeting Governor Pawlenty

I only had a few meetings with Governor Pawlenty when I was a House member, but I always thought it was a privilege, especially in the beginning. It didn't feel real; I was a legislator talking to the governor.

I knew that few people ever get to serve as a legislator. So each time I walked up the Capitol steps and into the House or Senate chambers, I was always in awe of the place. It was a privilege to serve.

The two-year budget in 2005 was not completed until we went all the way to a short-lived state government shutdown. In Minnesota, by constitution, the legislature must pass a budget, or the state government shuts down. So, unlike the federal legislature, where they continue to do CRs, or continuing resolutions, to fund government, Minnesota legislators must do their job and balance the budget. Even though it's hard, I wish the federal government had the same requirement.

The second year, 2006, seemed uneventful compared to the shouting matches in caucus the prior year. Some things did get done, but nothing had to be done in the second year of the two-year term. The bonding bill is usually the main focus to get done in the second year.

BONDING BILLS

In my early years as a legislator, I thought bonding bills for infrastructure were a waste of money. Over time I concluded that I would rather spend money on actual infrastructure than many other boondoggles. A bonding bill requires a super majority to pass, and that usually means that some extra votes are secured by placing a project in the bill that is in the district of a legislator who is wishy-washy about voting for a bonding bill but would vote for the bill if the project is in it. Sometimes these projects were a waste of money but necessary to pass the overall bill.

As I mentioned, the legislature is a pressure cooker for those that are serving there. There are times that marriage and family relationships are damaged because the legislator is away from his or her family for long periods of time. I was grateful that Maralee and I rented a house in the Twin Cities for our family and enrolled our children in a Christian school while I served at the Capitol. But even my marriage and family were strained by the heavy load of serving as a legislator. In those first two years, I felt like I had to be available for every call, whenever it was. It was like the phone was glued to my ear. That was not fair to my family, and looking back, I know it impacted them. I was not available to them enough, and I could have done better at balancing my work and family life.

GOD REALLY LIKES YOU

Other legislators were struggling too. Some drank more than they should have. Some got too close to individual lobbyists. I remember passing by a legislator one time during a floor session. As I walked by, I got the strong impression that the Lord really liked this legislator. It was an odd thought; I had never felt that about anyone before, that the Lord liked someone. I turned around and shared that impression with this legislator. The person's face went flush, and the person blurted out that they just slept with a lobbyist the night before. This person was married. Obviously there were troubled waters ahead for this legislator. Another legislator and I took time to pray for this person in a private area.

I thought about it afterward. In a person's worst moments, God still loved them. It really was a lesson for me in my own life, to treat people much more generously than I had been. As I read the four gospels, Matthew, Mark, Luke, and John, I saw Jesus constantly being warm to the ones society had rejected. He was considered a friend to the sinners and tax collectors—and politicians too, I will add.

My own Christian life as an adult was a bit sheltered, with time spent hanging out mostly with people just like me. As a legislator, however, I met people from many more walks of life. This gave me the opportunity to see more than what I had been seeing. Even though my personality is more driven, my hope has always been that people around me will see me as warm and friendly, even if we don't agree on everything. I want people to know that at their worst, they are still valuable, and I'm still a friend.

One person said that you really had to be bad for Gazelka not to like you. I took that as a compliment. The older I get, the softer I am toward the flaws of those around me. Maralee said that I had to be careful not to be sweeter than Jesus. After all, there was a time Jesus flipped over tables in righteous anger.

I think one of my favorite stories from the gospels is the story of a woman caught in adultery. The religious folks at the time threw her at the feet of Jesus. They reminded Him that their law said she should be stoned to death. Then they asked Jesus what He thought should happen to her. He said, "He who is without sin among you, let him throw a stone at her first" (John 8:7). What a surprise—no one cast the first stone. But what really stands out to me, as I have become older, is the folks who left the scene first where the older ones. The longer I have lived, the bigger the pile of stupid things I have done is, the more I'm grateful that my sins are forgiven by Jesus, and the more I want to be quick to forgive those around me.

If I'm going to err one way or the other in how I treat people, too soft or too hard, I would rather be considered too soft. Standing up for the right things matters, but you don't have to be a jerk while you do it. "A soft answer turns away wrath, but a harsh word stirs up anger" (Prov. 15:1).

MORE INFLUENCE

The first two years as a legislator gave me a lot more influence in my local community and in my role in ministry in various other places.

Praying in Parliament

In the summer of 2005 Maralee and I were traveling to London, England, for a business trip. It was a chartered flight and landed on the morning of July 7 at Kent International Airport, just outside of London. As the chartered bus we were riding in was heading toward London, all the overhead signs suddenly blared that London was closed. No one was getting into London. Our bus pulled over, and we sat there waiting to understand what was happening. London was closed! Coordinated suicide bombers detonated bombs on the London Underground. Two of the bombing locations were within a mile of the hotel we were scheduled to stay at. Our host said that anyone who didn't want to stay in London could get an immediate flight back to the United States. It was scary, but we decided to stay. I assumed that once the attacks happened, there would not be another. But I was wrong. A fourth bomber blew up a double-decker bus about an hour later.[4] However, we were not leaving.

It was a business trip, but while we were there, we decided to attend a local church that had been recommended to us. After the service ended, we talked to a few people, one of whom was Julie Anderson, one of the organizers of England's National Day of Prayer.

Once Julie found out I was a legislator from the US, she asked if we could attend their National Prayer Breakfast and church gathering after. They asked me to speak and pray at St. Stephen's Chapel, a seven-hundred-year-old church in the Palace of Westminster, where Parliament meets. What an amazing place! It had somehow survived all the wars and was still there.

At the prayer breakfast we rubbed shoulders with members of

Parliament, and Maralee and I had the opportunity to pray with one of their members. At the same time we were there, a piece of legislation, called the Racial and Religious Hatred Act, was being debated in the House of Commons.[5] If passed as was written at that time, it would have made it difficult for a person to publicly share their faith in the public square.

After the prayer breakfast, we watched the debate in the House of Commons gallery. It did pass the lower body that day, but it was modified in the House of Lords months later and did not prohibit publicly sharing about Jesus. I don't think it was a coincidence that we were there on the exact day an anti-Christian bill was being debated on the floor. We had the opportunity to agree in prayer with a gathering of Christians in St. Stephens Chapel. It was a privilege to be a part of this moment. The doors to participate in this experience opened because of my legislative position.

Bulgaria

The following year, I was in Bulgaria on a ministry trip. I met their former prime minister because of my role as a state legislator. He wasn't sure if I was a state legislator or national legislator. In the end, when he found out I was from a state, he was not quite as interested. Having said that, I'm pretty sure the GDP of Minnesota is greater than that of Bulgaria...but who keeps track?

SESSION DONE, TIME TO MOVE BACK HOME

We moved back home after the end of the session in May of 2005. It was great to be home, but it was different. Because we moved our family to the Twin Cities during session from January to May, we did not go home on most weekends. Our kids were plugging into a new school and friends, and if they preferred to stay in the Twin Cities over the weekend, I wanted to be flexible. So when we went home for the second half of the year, we had to catch up on life and our friends. Life had not stopped while we were gone.

Then we sent our kids to school in the Brainerd area in late August for the first half of the next school year. That was an adjustment for them as well. This was not a perfect arrangement, but all of us were trying to make it work. We decided that after the Christmas school break, we would move back to our Brooklyn Center rental house and enroll our kids again at the same school. This was our pattern from year to year.

It was in that second school year in the Twin Cities that a couple of our kids started to struggle. That made the balance between work and family almost impossible to navigate. The struggles were beyond our parenting abilities, and we sought professional counseling for help.

It was already hard enough for me to balance all of my responsibilities with a work schedule in my insurance agency in Brainerd and my legislative responsibilities at the Capitol. But with kids struggling at the same time, I wasn't sure what to do. Maralee was also at the breaking point.

Then, when it didn't seem as if it could be any worse, we got notice from our landlord that we needed to be out of the house in two weeks. They had sold the house.

MARALEE'S FRANTIC PRAYER FOR A HOUSE

I was right in the middle of the session. I had no time to manage this impossible request. Maralee's frantic prayer was that we would find a house on a lake, fully furnished, that would be even better than the place we were living in.

Sure enough, a lady at the church we were attending in Brooklyn Park heard about our plight and mentioned that she was going to be spending six months in Florida, and if we wanted, we could rent her house during the time she was gone. It happened to be on a lake, fully furnished, and better than the place we were living in.

It was the toughest family season of our life, but God was providing for us in the midst of the storm.

RUNNING FOR REELECTION
TO THE HOUSE

As the two-year term was winding down, I ramped up my campaign for reelection. I assumed I would win. I did all the same hard work, and I knew much more. But I did not win. John Ward, a former teacher, was my opponent. He was well organized and popular. My House GOP team never dreamed I would lose and did not focus much on my race. I thought the race was going well, but Ward seemed to be building momentum too. I was known as a big supporter of the business community, I served as vice chairman of the Commerce Committee, and I was receiving legislative awards acknowledging my legislative work from the business community.

It was a complete surprise when Walmart asked me if I would give public remarks at an event honoring their Teacher of the Year recipient, John Ward. Normally that would be a great opportunity for me, but they gave my political opponent the Teacher of the Year award. That award gave him front page press in our local newspaper weeks in front of the election. I decided to make the best of it and gave positive remarks about John Ward, the teacher. As I got up to speak, the John Ward crowd was on the edge of their seats. What would I say? I simply smiled and started my public comments by saying, "Stranger things have happened to me..." The crowd was put at ease, and the speech was well received. But a month later John Ward defeated me in my House race.

I thought I was going to win. We had nearly one thousand signs up in people's yards. We put over half of the signs up over one weekend. I called it the shock-and-awe approach. I felt I did well in the televised debates and had an answer for every tricky question. But sometimes you think you're going to win, and you don't win. That's politics in a swing district. After I had put in all the hard work and served as the legislator for my district, the loss was painful. My dad had passed away the year before, and the political defeat felt about the same emotionally. My heart was emotionally invested in serving my community, and within a few hours after the election polls closed, I went from thinking I would remain a legislator to losing to my political challenger. The agony of defeat was more than I expected. It's a weird feeling running for political office. You put everything on the line, and sometimes you lose and then feel rejected.

PROTECT TEEN CHALLENGE PROJECT

After the election I asked John Ward to meet me for coffee at a local coffee shop in Brainerd. It was tough to lose, but John was going to be the new representative for our area. I had been working on a project to help Minnesota Adult and Teen Challenge expand in the Brainerd Lakes area. I wanted John Ward to know how important the project would be for our area and asked him to help the project get done. Teen Challenge is the most successful drug and rehabilitation program in the state of Minnesota. Men and women that go through their program have a 75 percent success rate of being free of alcohol and drug addiction five years after graduating from the program. The Christ-centered program works. The rest of the government-run programs have about a 25 percent success rate after five years.

I was grateful that John continued the effort to help the program start in Brainerd, and when the time came for Teen Challenge to open their facility in Brainerd, John Ward made it a point to tell the exuberant crowd that I had been the one to initially shepherd the project through the legislative process. He did not have to do that but chose to.

OFFENDED LGBTQ SENATOR

I had the opportunity to intervene several times at the Capitol for Teen Challenge over my years as a legislator. One time, a legislator wanted to remove a million dollars of state funding from Teen Challenge because they were a Christian group that supported a biblical worldview on marriage and family issues.[6] That is not what they focus on in their program, but it is what they believe. The legislator, who was part of the LGBTQ community, was offended by their position.

I was grateful that I had a good working relationship with Representative John Ward. Together we approached Governor Dayton privately and made our case for the full funding for Teen Challenge, and in the end, they were fully funded.

Later I attended a gala dinner fundraising event for Teen Challenge in Minneapolis. As I was singing a worship song along with the Teen Challenge choir, I started thinking about the LGBTQ legislator and how some Christians must have treated him wrongly. I pictured myself apologizing to him on behalf of the Christians that did not treat him well.

The next day, when I was at the Capitol, I decided that I would tell him about my thoughts from the night before. I went to his office and asked if I could talk to him privately. We were a bit like water and oil over the years, so he was hesitant, but he brought me back to his office anyway. I shared the story about picturing him mistreated by Christians in his past. Then I said, "On behalf of those Christians, I want to apologize to you."

He appreciated what I said and did. We talked a bit about his religious upbringing as well, and then we both went about our legislative day.

I believe in the Holy Scriptures and endeavor to live my life by them. I also try to respond to what I believe are promptings from the Lord that compel me to reach out to people with the love of God. I don't do it perfectly; I just try to do my best. In this situation I think it made a difference.

LOST REELECTION TO JOHN WARD—DONE WITH POLITICS?

Because of all that was going on in our personal life, Maralee was relieved that I lost. She supported me, but the toll on our marriage and family was too much. I had not figured out the work-life balance in this season of our lives. I felt my role in the legislature was important, maybe even too important. Too often the family was not on the front burner of my priorities. That doesn't mean I was absent, but I simply couldn't figure out how to make it all fit well.

The House was not a perfect fit for me either because of how I am made. It was full of emotion and fighting, and as an entity, it was in constant election mode. I prefer a more reasoned approach. I don't like to force myself into a conversation, which is what it felt like I had to do in the House floor debates and in our large caucus discussions. I also did not like constant campaigning. The House is by design a different body than the Senate. But when I lost my House race, I thought I was done. I had no grand plans to run again. It was a huge sacrifice to my family and to my business.

I thought I was done with government, but just like in the beginning, even if I wasn't looking for politics, politics was looking for me.

CHAPTER 2

CLIMBING EAGLE MOUNTAIN—BACK IN POLITICS

Acouple of years went by, and we mostly settled back into normal life. But politics and issues took on a new meaning. I had been in the trenches, so now I knew how things worked. I had been there.

Maralee carried the pain of my two years serving in the House. Two of our teenage children really struggled emotionally during those two years. Maralee had to bear more of that responsibility than if I had not been a legislator. She was glad I was out of politics and not looking to get back in.

ACCIDENTALLY STAY AT HOTEL WHERE GOP CONVENTION IS HELD

Then our son had a soccer tournament in the Twin Cities. We booked a random hotel near the tournament. As we went to check into the hotel, we started running into Republican activists and legislators that we knew. We were not sure what was going on, but it was odd. As it turned out, the Republican Party of Minnesota was having their state meeting at the same hotel we had booked for our son's soccer tournament. I had really backed way off of my involvement in party politics, and suddenly it was thrust in our faces.

I looked at Maralee and told her I really didn't know this political event was going to be at the hotel I booked. She knew I was telling the truth, but we both had to wonder if the Lord was up to something.

After a bit more time went by, we wondered if we should consider running for the Minnesota Senate. We had a Republican state senator in our area, but he was pushing an agenda that was contrary to Republican positions. It was tricky; he had announced that he was gay, but he said he supported traditional marriage. But because I was also serving in the House at the time, I knew that was not true. That was an important issue to me. Maralee and I had done a lot of ministry to married couples. I was willing to support civil unions for gay couples, but I didn't think they should have the right to redefine marriage. I heard enough difficult stories from gay couples about situations they encountered as a result of not being married but just living together—like not being able to have visitation rights in a hospital. Civil unions would have solved all of these situations.

For most in the LGBTQ community, that was not enough; they wanted marriage. Years later, the US Supreme Court settled the issue for the entire country and ruled that any two people can marry. That does not line up with my biblical worldview, but it is the decision that was made for our country.

As we continued to contemplate whether I should run for the Senate, Maralee went to a Christian women's event. They announced that they were going to have a surprise guest speaker— Congresswoman Michele Bachmann. Maralee knew Michele from our work with her on various issues while she served in the state senate. But Maralee was at a Christian women's conference, not a political one. Again, we both felt that God was tugging us back into politics. Both Bachmann and another prominent speaker encouraged Maralee to engage again in politics.

MIRACLE RENDEZVOUS AT EAGLE MOUNTAIN

Unless Maralee and I both agreed that I should run again, I was unwilling to do so. We took a trip to the north shore of Lake Superior. As we were sitting in the hotel in Canal Park in Duluth, Minnesota, we thought about hiking to the top of Eagle Mountain, the highest peak in Minnesota. We thought we could take the time to pray for Minnesota while we were up on top of the mountain. We had never been there before, but we decided we were going to do it.

Within a few hours, Dan Hall, a chaplain at the Minnesota Capitol, called us up to ask if we knew anywhere on the north shore of Lake Superior that he could stay with for a night. He had plans to climb Eagle Mountain to pray for Minnesota.

What are the odds? Within a few hours of each other, we all felt like we should climb Eagle Mountain. None of us had ever climbed it before, and we have not climbed it since.

It was a long hike to the top and worth it. The vista views were mostly to the interior, and they were spectacular. We found the geological marker, and together we prayed for Minnesota. Little did we know then that within a year and a half, Dan Hall and I would both be Minnesota state senators.

We made the decision a little while later to run against the sitting Republican senator. I didn't realize that plenty of GOP folks did not like the fact that I was challenging a sitting Republican senator, but we felt like it was the right thing to do. We announced our intention on October 1, 2009, my birthday, with a fundraiser for the race. We started to raise money right away and invited people to come and bring fifty dollars for me on my fiftieth birthday, another of Maralee's ideas.

We formed a new campaign with a new campaign manager, Joyce Heffron. Joyce and her family peppered me with questions about where I stood on issues, especially social issues. If they were going to get involved with my campaign, they wanted to know I was the real deal. When they decided they would help, I had no idea that meant 120 percent effort, especially from Joyce, her daughters Mandy and Janaya, and her husband, Loren.

The Heffrons introduced us to Ken and Ruby Toenies, another key couple who volunteered on our campaign team. Among many responsibilities, they oversaw getting our signs up around the district.

The sitting Republican senator had been challenged by a fellow Republican in the prior election but survived that challenge. I engaged early in my challenge to defeat him. First, I outworked him for the Republican endorsement, so he skipped the endorsement meeting. Instead, he ran directly to the primary, where he had bested his previous GOP challenger. As the primary day approached, he had to decide whether he would run as an independent or a Republican. If he chose to run as a Republican and lost the primary, he was out. If he chose to run as an independent, he was on the ballot all the way to November and made it nearly impossible for me to win, but it would also be difficult for him to win.

He locked into running as a Republican, a decision that could not be changed after a certain date before the primary. As it turned out, just after that date was reached, he had dinner with a gay porn star in a local restaurant in the Brainerd area. His dinner guest tweeted about the dinner, and it ended up becoming a significant news story.[1] This dinner date activity was too extreme for the local Republicans. As a result of this event, I ended up winning the primary and he was out—or so I thought.

Keep in mind this was a swing district at the time, which meant the people sometimes select a Republican legislator to represent them, and sometimes they select a Democrat legislator to represent them.

To defeat the sitting incumbent Republican senator, well-meaning outside groups spent money independently from me, highlighting the news story about the dinner with the gay porn star. The ads were slimy and embarrassing. Independent expenditures are just that—independent of the candidate and his campaign. Had I known about them, I would not have approved of them. Our campaign approach was to speak respectfully about the Republican senator we were challenging and simply focus on the issues we were different on. The senator's lack of judgment regarding the newsworthy dinner sunk his own ship.

But when I won the primary over the sitting Republican senator, it did not sit well with him. He knew he was not going to be reelected but decided to launch a write-in campaign for people to vote for him in the November election instead of me, siphoning votes away from me.

In this race there was also a candidate representing the Constitution Party, a right-leaning political party. This person had volunteered on my earlier race for the House seat and now wanted to run himself. His decision to run meant that 1 or 2 percent of voters who would normally vote for a Republican candidate would be siphoned away to him by his entrance into the race. That would make the race even closer.

As it turned out, the Democrats fielded a candidate that was just out of college and therefore perceived as not ready for the job. He did worse than prior Democrat candidates had done. So as the election ended, the sitting senator got about 10 percent of the vote as a write-in candidate, the Constitution Party candidate got about 2 percent of the vote, and I somehow still won the election.

That election, in November of 2010, was a wave election for Republicans. It was so big that for the first time in forty years, Republicans took the Senate majority in Minnesota. There were thirty-seven Republican senators, twenty-one of whom were brand new, and there were thirty Democratic senators. It was a huge seat change that I'm certain many assumed was impossible. The credit really goes to Senator Dave Senjem and his newly hired political staffer, Mike Campbell. It had been a long time since Republicans had really tried to win the majority, and somehow their work, in a wave election, was enough to do the impossible.

CHAPTER 3

OPENING HOUSE PRAYER THAT ROCKED THE CAPITOL

T HE ELECTION OF 2010 was a watershed moment for Republicans. They won both the Senate and the House in Minnesota. The Senate had not been under Republican control in over forty years. We didn't win by just one vote; it was 37–30.

The GOP Senate win in 2010 was remarkable. It took a little bit of luck and a big wave election. But it also would not have happened if Dave Senjem had not believed it could happen.

Senator Senjem was the Republican minority leader in 2010. Before his leadership, there was little belief that Republicans could actually win the majority in the Senate, but Dave believed they could.

He charted a different course from prior leaders. He hired Mike Campbell as his political director, and Mike also thought they could win. They had virtually no campaign money because no one wanted to give them money when it was assumed they would just lose anyway.

Mike Campbell took out a loan for $100,000 for the Senate Republican campaign and personally guaranteed it. Now that is confidence—or utter insanity. Later, when I became leader and found out about it, I told him never to do that again. But that is how committed he was to winning.

So with a team that believed they could, with candidates that believed they could, and a GOP wave, the unthinkable happened. Republicans took the majority in the Minnesota Senate.

AMY KOCH IS FIRST REPUBLICAN MAJORITY LEADER IN MODERN TIMES

Amy Koch became the first Republican majority leader elected in Minnesota. Before the mid-1970s, there was no party designation in the Senate, and once party designations began, Republicans had never won the Senate majority. In addition to being the first Republican majority leader, Koch was also the first woman in Minnesota from either party to become majority leader.

Senator Michelle Fischbach became the president of the Senate, the first woman from either party to take that position. Senator Claire Robling became the chair of the most powerful committee, the Finance Committee, and she also was the first woman in that position. Senator Julianne Ortman became the chair of the Taxes Committee, and she also was the first woman in that position.

Republicans in the Senate led the way, putting women in the four most powerful positions. Republicans, at times, are accused as a party of not supporting women. But actions speak louder than words, and our actions in the Senate were to put the most qualified people—in this case, four women—in the four most powerful positions.

As I mentioned, in the 2010 elections, Republicans won both legislative houses. Winning both houses meant that we could actually pass bills that clearly showed what our agenda was and send them to the governor's desk. If one body is controlled by Democrats, and the other body is controlled by Republicans, neither side gets to really show what their agenda would have been because the two bodies had to compromise before sending the bill for the governor's signature.

This was a unique moment for the Republicans in the Senate, and it was going to be difficult for our selected leader, Amy Koch, to govern well. Of the thirty-seven Republican senators, twenty-one were freshmen, or brand new. Some of us, like Scott Newman and me, had served in the House and were "House trained," as the House liked to say. But most of the new Republican senators had no legislative experience.

I was fortunate in that I already had two years of legislative experience as part of a majority. I was ready to go. Ken Swecker was my predecessor's legislative assistant. I debated whether it would be wise for me to have him work for me, in that he might still be loyal to the senator I just defeated. That was not the case. Ken worked diligently for several years for me before he went back to school for additional training.

In the House, legislators are seated to the right and left in their chamber. In the Senate, the minority sits in the front, and the majority sits in the back. I was seated in the very back row on the left.

$6 BILLION DEFICIT

Our new GOP Senate majority did better than most expected, but not as well as we could have done. We were saddled with the difficult task of balancing a budget that projected to be $6 billion short.[1] And we were dead set against raising taxes.

Mark Dayton was the Democratic governor, and he did not want to decrease government spending, for sure not by $6 billion.

In my first year as a freshman senator, I was the vice chair of the Senate Commerce Committee. I built good relationships with many of the legislators on the Commerce Committee. It should not have been a surprise, but I was surprised at the insight from some of the Democratic legislators on the committee, like James Metzen and Roger Reinert. I encountered the same surprise on the Environment Committee. Democratic Senator Rod Skoe was talking about tree-climbing deer stands, and I found myself agreeing with his perspective. If it made sense, I was not opposed to incorporating their ideas into what we were doing as the majority. That's what I would have wanted done if I had been in the minority.

I also discovered that one particular Democratic senator was given no help by the Republican chair of a particular committee. I didn't understand why none of this senator's ideas, even when they made sense, were listened to. I found out that this particular senator, when he was in the majority, did similar things to the Republican senator when Republicans were in the minority, and he was now reaping what he sowed.

The 2011 session pitted a new Republican House and Senate majority against Democratic Governor Dayton. Everyone was dug in. We wanted to pass a whole agenda worth of reforms, but Governor Dayton stood in the way.

TRADITIONAL MARRIAGE AMENDMENT

In the same year, at the same time, Republicans were moving two constitutional amendments forward to be on the ballot in November of 2012. One of them was the traditional marriage amendment. The marriage amendment had become an epic struggle. For years attempts were made to protect traditional marriage in Minnesota. Now, because Republicans controlled the House and Senate, the ability to pass a constitutional amendment was possible.

What was going on in Minnesota was happening across the country. Thirty-one states already had amendments affirming that marriage was only between a man and a woman.

OPENING HOUSE PRAYER THAT ROCKED THE CAPITOL

This was one of the most emotional issues I had to address in my political career. Just as the vote on the marriage amendment was ready to happen in the House, a rocker turned preacher, Bradlee Dean, came to give the opening prayer of the House. To many, his prayer was perceived as hell-fire condemnation. Legislative opening prayers are not meant to be a teaching or chastisement of the legislative bodies, and at this moment, his words were akin to a bomb being tossed in the room.

Either Bradlee Dean didn't get the message on expectations for legislative opening prayers, or he chose to use the moment to make his point. Either way, his prayer almost killed the traditional marriage amendment.

Speaker Kurt Zellers was livid. He seethed that if Bradlee Dean came back to the Capitol, the marriage amendment was done.

Recess was called in the House to calm everyone down. Maralee, Senator Dan Hall, and I heard about the dustup while taking a lunch break offsite. We wondered what the final outcome would be, but we really wanted to get the marriage amendment to the people for a vote. We had heard about Zeller's comments as well.

DIVINE INTERVENTION

As we were coming back to the Capitol, we were about to park in front under the quadriga (the four golden horses on top of the Capitol)—a senatorial privilege at the time—and noticed Bradlee Dean approaching the front steps of the Capitol. We quickly drove our car down to him as he was placing his foot on the first step. I rolled down my window and asked him what he was doing. He said that he was not treated right and was coming back to clear his name in a press conference. We had the opportunity to share with him that if he did that, the marriage amendment would fail. I asked him what he thought was more important, and in the end, he left without doing the press conference.

I'm sure it was tough for him. He came to do a chaplain's prayer, something he had not done at the Capitol before, and he was lambasted. But he swallowed his pride and left the Capitol complex, and the amendment came before both bodies and passed.

ANOTHER GOVERNMENT SHUTDOWN

In 2011 Minnesota experienced the longest shutdown in its history, and it was a result of stubbornness on both sides.

We had a firm stance on new taxes: "not a penny more." We were committed to not raising taxes, and we were willing to aggressively cut government spending instead. We passed balanced budgets that did not require a tax increase and sent them to the governor's desk near the end of session. It should not have been a surprise, but the governor vetoed much of what went to his desk.

Nobody wanted to budge, and we ended up in the longest state government shutdown in Minnesota history.

Finally the dam broke, and the governor caved to much of what we demanded.

When the shutdown finally ended, it felt at first like we had won. We got more of our policies through than the governor wanted, and a budget that initially was projected to have a $6 billion shortfall was balanced without raising taxes. All of that was very good.

We put two constitutional amendments on the November 2012 ballot—one required a photo ID to vote, and the second one affirmed that marriage was only between a man and a woman. The governor did not support either of these initiatives, which meant that we would not get them done through the legislative process. So we decided to let the people decide through the constitutional amendment process, which only requires the House and Senate to agree.

This process does not require the governor's approval and is instead determined by the people through the ballot process. The second benefit of a constitutional amendment is that the supreme court of that state cannot say something is unconstitutional if the people voted for it to be part of their constitution. For clarity, the US Supreme Court can override a state supreme court position or a state constitution position.

INSTEAD OF TRADITIONAL MARRIAGE, GAY MARRIAGE BECOMES THE LAW

In the end, in November of 2012 at the ballot box, Minnesota was the first state where the traditional marriage amendment failed. The following year, gay marriage passed the legislative bodies in Minnesota when Democrats took complete control. And a bit after that, the US Supreme Court decided to overrule thirty-one state marriage amendments and declared gay marriage would be allowed across the United States.

FIRST MEETING WITH GOVERNOR DAYTON

In that first year, just after the session finished in May, Governor Dayton was visiting the college in my district. Maralee and I both felt like we should offer to meet the governor for coffee. I had no idea whether he would take me up on the request, but he did. In fact, when he came into the coffee shop, he told his staff that he wanted to meet alone with us. That made the meeting much more personal.

We started off the conversation saying we thought he would benefit from a few Republican friends, just like I benefited from having a few Democratic friends in the Senate. The conversation was about our personal lives. The whole thing surprised me, but it was an important meeting for future conflicts between the governor and the Republicans controlling the Senate and the House when I was the Senate leader.

In my second year, I became one of six assistant majority leaders. Because there were so many new people, the opportunities for leadership were much more available than normal for a freshman.

Even so, much of the decision making was still made by a few experienced leaders. We were an inexperienced group that needed more experience fast. We were idealistic but really didn't fully understand how difficult it would be to come to an agreement with a Democratic governor heading a much different direction.

When making the decision to put two questions on a ballot for the people to decide, we didn't fully understand the amount of money that would flow into the state to defeat these initiatives, especially the marriage amendment. Early polling data showed that the public supported our positions on both of these issues. But those that supported these initiatives did not have the financial resources to compete with those that wanted to defeat these initiatives. Money flooded into the state from those that wanted the marriage amendment defeated, and in the end, both ballot initiatives failed. The primary reason they failed was because of a masterful campaign from the opposition who produced very well-done ads and combined the separate groups together to simply vote no on both questions.

These ballot initiatives were going to impact the turnout for the general election because they would be voted on at the same time legislators and statewide office holders were up for election.

In addition our selected majority leader of that time had an inappropriate sexual relationship with one of the Senate GOP employees under this person's leadership. As a result this leader ended up being forced to step down as majority leader when the improper relationship came to light. That Senate GOP moment wasn't fun for anyone, and I'm glad I didn't have a role in any of that matter. GOP friends suddenly became adversaries. It was a no-win situation for everyone.

In the election of 2012 the combination of all the things mentioned sent a message to Minnesotans that caused them to reelect enough Democrat legislators in the Senate to allow them to take back the Senate majority. Minnesota is a left-leaning state, and on some occasions, we are purple at best. I often say that for Republicans to win in Minnesota, they can't make any mistakes. Coming up to the elections of November 2012, we made too many mistakes.

For a brief two years of a forty-two year span, Republicans held the majority in the Senate, but that was now gone. Democrats now won the House, Senate, and governorship, and with this complete trifecta, they erased everything we had accomplished. It was painful to watch. They passed large tax increases, dramatically increased government spending, and eliminated many of the reforms we had enacted. One reform we enacted was the Sunset Commission. This commission was tasked with reviewing every agency and state board, over a ten-year period, to see if they were still necessary or too bloated and needed reform. The commission functioned for one year and showed promise to rein in waste. But with a complete takeover by Democrats, one of the first decisions they made was to sunset the Sunset Commission. It was hard to watch our hard-fought reforms go up in smoke, but that is the nature and consequences of total swings in political power.

CHAPTER 4

A VIVID WARNING DREAM

EVERY TEN YEARS the boundaries for Senate districts are redrawn to reflect population changes. It's called redistricting. My district ended up changing a lot. In my own race for reelection to the Senate, with redistricting, my district had become more vulnerable to a challenge from Democrats. In addition, there were rumblings that the prior Republican senator might run as an independent, assuring my defeat by dividing the Republican vote.

A new district had formed just a few miles from where I lived that leaned much more conservative, and it did not have a sitting senator in it. Part of this district included Morrison County, which was part of my old district. It made sense to move there, but it would be a hassle for my family, and I was in the mood to stay and fight.

I was undecided on what to do, but my wife, Maralee; my legislative assistant, Ken Swecker; and others were concerned that I would not win reelection if I remained where I was.

As I was about to make a decision, I woke up from a vivid dream about Demos Shakarian, the founder of a prominent international ministry. His family had lived in Armenia and Russia and emigrated from there to California at the beginning of the 1900s. That move was prompted by a vision a prophet had of tragedy coming to their people and that they must flee to a place of refuge. This was a warning from the Lord about something that came to pass; thousands did die, were exiled, or were persecuted for their faith not long after the dream.[1]

I was dreaming about this story. I may not even have all the correct facts about it, but that was what I was dreaming about when I woke up. Then, in that quiet, early-morning moment, I felt like the Lord was saying to me, "I've asked you to move into the other district. If you don't move, there will be a plan to take you out."

I shared that thought and dream with Maralee, and we both came to the decision that we should move into the district with an open seat. We sold our precious home on Gilbert Lake and moved ten miles to the west. It was an emotionally hard move for us; we loved our home and all the memories it held. We ended up finding a beautiful home that was listed as a short sale in the new district and decided to buy it rather than rent a place. We were not pretending to move; we moved!

There are times that during redistricting a legislator will rent an apartment and claim it as his permanent address so that he can serve in that district. More than once a legislator has been busted for not really living in the district he plans to represent, and I was not going to do that. Finding a nice home softened the pain of leaving our dream home, and in the end, we knew it was the right move. So in a Democratic wave election, when Republicans went back into the minority, I easily won my bid for reelection in this new district.

Prophetic Declaration—Ruud Will Be a Senator Again

Carrie Ruud decided to run again for the Senate in my old district, the one I moved away from. Even that election was an answer from the Lord. Carrie had been a senator but was defeated in her reelection years earlier. She was still at the Capitol as a lobbyist. At that time, Maralee had invited Dave Duell to come down and minister to folks at the Capitol. Dave often prayed and spoke pro-phetic words over the people he encountered. At least a year before redistricting, Dave Duell spoke a prophetic word to Carrie Ruud that she would be back at the Capitol as a senator again.

I couldn't see how that would happen as Carrie lived in a dis-trict that Republicans already were serving in. But as the Senate boundaries were redrawn, Carrie was in the district I was moving out of. I never even thought about Dave Duell's prayer over Carrie. I called Carrie to tell her I was moving out of my district and said that she might consider running for that seat. After she said yes, my thoughts returned to Dave Duell's prayer declaration over her, that she would be a senator again. Where I once thought there was no way it would happen, now I thought it would truly happen, and it came to pass. Carrie Ruud fit the district much better than I did, and she did not have personal opposition from the former Republican senator that I had defeated.

RUUD CONFRONTS WITH GRACE AND TRUTH

Here is a story I love about Carrie Ruud that is worth sharing. Sometime after she won her election in 2012, she was sitting at a committee table next to a Democratic senator who was scrolling through pornographic material on his phone. He didn't know she could see his phone. She was irritated at his unprofessional behavior. Later she asked my advice about what to do about it. I wasn't the leader then, but I asked her what outcome she was looking for. If she wanted to make the Democrats look bad, and this senator in par-ticular, she could file a formal complaint. If she thought his actions did not reflect well on the entire Senate, she could approach him privately and tell him how she felt. She chose the latter direction.

She wasn't trying to make him look bad; she just wanted him to be more professional. So she decided to approach him privately and share her concerns with him. He appreciated her approach and took her advice to heart. She was acting like a stateswoman.

In the Minority, but God Says Act Like I'm in the Majority

As I returned to the Senate after my reelection victory, I found myself completely in the minority. In my prayer time with the Lord about this, I felt like He impressed upon my heart to act like I was in the majority. Godly people of old—like Daniel, Joseph, and Esther—all served and influenced kingdoms while being the minority. Why couldn't I do the same?

I was so glad that the two years earlier, when I was in the majority, I treated Democratic senators in the minority the way I would have wanted to be treated if I was in their shoes. If they had a good idea, I honored it. I tried to value them and their ideas. As a result, in the minority, I was still influential. I was able to pass legislation to get rid of the income tax on military pensions. I served on the Tax Conference Committee, learning how to negotiate with the House. And I built powerful relationships across the aisle with some of the Democratic leaders.

One particular relationship was with Senator Jim Metzen, the Commerce Committee chair. I was the lead Republican on the Commerce Committee. Jim had been a banker before serving in the Senate. My background was insurance. Both of these industries were often part of the Commerce Committee discussions. We played off each other. We both were heading in the same general direction. We got to a point where lobbyists would approach Senator Metzen, and he would ask them what I thought. When the lobbyists approached me on an issue, I would ask them what Metzen thought. It really reflected how government could work, and it worked well.

Some committees have much more divisive issues, and it's even more difficult to find common ground between two opposing sides. Even so, it's worth the effort to start with respect and look for opportunities to agree among the many areas of disagreement. Republican Senator Jim Abeler and Democratic Senator John Hoffman served the Senate well by having this type of relationship on the Health and Human Services Committee. Republican Senator Warren Limmer formed a respectful relationship with Democratic Senator Ron Latz on the Judiciary Committee. In all these connections, there was often disagreement, but because of mutual respect, they found places to work together.

DEMOCRATIC SENATOR METZEN'S HEALTH FAILING—HEAVEN IS NEAR

Senator Metzen was in his last term because his health was failing. We became friends. I hated to see him drifting away. We had a break on one of the last days of the session, and the two of us were up in his office at the Capitol. At that time, offices for senators in the minority were in the State Office Building, and offices for senators in the majority were in the Capitol. I knew that I wasn't going to have many more conversations with Jim Metzen, my friend. As we sat there alone in his office, our conversation led to eternal questions, life after this life ends. It was reassuring to me that Senator Metzen affirmed his faith in Jesus as his Savior. When all your chips are down, what really matters is where you will spend eternity. Jim declared his faith.

As we returned to the Senate floor from the session break, it was Senator Metzen's turn to give his retirement speech. He talked about the many friends he had in the Senate, including me, and all the good memories he had serving. I wasn't Jim's best friend, but we had just talked about eternity, and it obviously meant a lot to him. I know I will see him again. The time comes for all of us to leave this earth, and like Jim, I also believe in Jesus as my Savior. And Jesus said that He has prepared a place in eternity for all those that believe and trust in Him as their Savior.

Senator Rod Skoe, a wild-rice farmer from north central Minnesota, was the Tax Committee chair during that time. We had united on various common-sense issues related to the Department of Natural Resources in prior years. But as I served on the Tax Committee with him, I realized that he was much more moderate on tax issues than many other Democrats. Democratic Senator Ann Rest was also on this committee. Because our Republican tax lead was running for higher office, her focus as Republican tax lead was less than normal. As a result I was the Republican they looked to in crafting a bill with Republican input, and I was the Republican selected to serve on the Tax Conference Committee to hash out tax language differences with the House.

For years I had been advocating for the elimination of the tax on military pensions. Anyone that has served twenty years in the armed forces qualifies for a pension. Many of these veterans will have a whole new career in front of them after they retire from the military. They are given information when they retire from the armed forces as to which states treat veterans best, and Minnesota was not one of the best states. Minnesota was an outlier on taxing military pensions.

As we were nearing the end of session that year, Senator Skoe asked me in private what my number one tax priority was. I told him it was to get rid of the tax on military pensions. Sure enough, when the tax bill was put together, the tax on military pensions, which was my SF40 bill, was eliminated. What I could not get done while in the majority got done with bipartisan effort while serving in the minority. It was a decent tax bill that I was asked to give input on. When we finished the tax bill, Senator Rest, a stickler for good tax policy and procedure, gave me a small piece of her Christmas cactus as a token of appreciation for the hard work I did. The cactus it came from was over a hundred years old, she said. Sharing a piece of it with me was her tradition to acknowledge good work done on the tax bill.

Senator Rest and I butted heads years earlier when Republicans first took the majority in 2011. I used the term Obamacare before it was acknowledged by President Obama as a positive term. She chastised me, reminding me that senators were meant to be more dignified in our approach. At the time, it irritated me, but as the years went by, I realized that our words do matter, and senators are meant to lead by example. In the end we became friends. Even after

I left the Senate, I went down to visit her to encourage better policy on a tax bill. I was welcomed into her office because I had earned that right as someone seeking the best tax policy for Minnesota, and I was a friend.

I also built a good relationship on the Commerce Committee with Senator Roger Reinert, a Democratic senator from Duluth. We sat next to each other and would periodically discuss issues privately while at the committee table. Sometimes we agreed, and sometimes we disagreed, but it was always respectful.

REINERT'S CHALLENGE COIN

Later Roger Reinert retired from the Senate and gave me his challenge coin. Senator Reinert was a Navy man. Military, police officers, and the like often exchange coins with each other. It never really meant much to me until Roger gave me his coin. Years earlier a military chaplain came to the Senate and did the opening prayer. I met the chaplain in the Senate retiring room after the prayer, and he gave me his coin, what I now know to be a challenge coin. The chaplain's coin had a Roman soldier on the front with a scripture from the Book of Ephesians, chapter 6, on the back. He gave it to me because he knew I was standing up for traditional family values and religious freedom, and it was his way of saying thank you and to keep up the fight.

So now Senator Roger Reinert gave me his challenge coin, and I had become aware of the significance of the power of exchanging challenge coins. I went to my apartment that night and found the Roman soldier challenge coin. The next day, on the Senate floor, I motioned Roger to come over to me. I gave him my challenge coin and shared how and why I got it, and that I wanted Roger to have it. We both felt the power of the exchange. That exchange was the beginning of a closer friendship with Roger from that time forward. A few weeks after the session ended, I got a letter in the mail at home from Roger with another Roman soldier challenge coin. He knew how important it was to me and wanted me to have another one. We shared similar faith in God, and this coin exchange created a bond that is still strong today. It doesn't mean we agree on everything, but it does mean we have a strong bond of friendship.

After that coin exchange I ordered a large batch of Roman soldier coins with the Scripture verse on the back. It has become my challenge coin to share with others. I have had the privilege of sharing the challenge coin with governors, a president and vice president, police officers, legislators from both parties, and the like. Almost every time I share the coin, it is a moving experience, helping form a deeper bond as a result.

MINORITY IS HARD TO ENDURE

I hated being part of the minority for four years. During the first two years of the minority, Democrats had the trifecta—governor, House, and Senate. They could do almost anything they wanted to do. The only thing that stopped them was a few moderate Democrat legislators who tempered extreme views from the Left.

In the last two years in the minority, the House was recaptured by Republicans, but even then, we felt like our voice in the Senate was of little significance. Too often the minority caucus in either the Senate or the House is the forgotten one. They can't do much, and often their perspective is not sought out.

We often whined about the fact that the media never cared much about what we had to say, but when the leaders of either the House or Senate showed up, a scrum formed.

While in the minority, I was civil with all the Democratic members of the Senate, but I had really good working relationships with about seven of them. As a result I occasionally was able to thwart some of their more progressive agenda items. I would quietly circle to the group of seven to see if there was any possibility of defeating a bill, and occasionally we did. Small victories were better than nothing. My alliances were mostly with freshmen Democratic senators from moderate districts, but over time, they became less flexible. Without those relationships though, I believe the Democratic majority would have been able to do even more of their party's progressive agenda.

MARALEE BELIEVES I WILL BECOME THE MAJORITY LEADER

At the end of those four years in the minority and with the November 2016 election coming up, I had just about enough of serving in the minority in the Senate. It felt like what a wild lion must feel like getting captured and sitting in a zoo for years. Eventually you can lose sight of who you are, the king of the jungle.

I had some success in the minority, but it is not the same as being in charge. I was contemplating when I might depart from the Senate. It was a lot easier running my insurance agency, and I got paid a lot more to do that.

As those thoughts were rolling around in my head at the end of the summer in 2016, Maralee began to sense a different path for me. She told me a few months before the election that she thought we were going to take the majority back and that I would be the majority leader. She said this at least a half dozen times in the next few months.

Winning the majority was possible; we had done it once in the last forty-six years. But becoming the majority leader seemed impossible. Our minority leader, David Hann, oversaw the elections, and if we took the majority, I would be supporting him for the Senate leader position.

Ten days before the election, Maralee asked me if I was calling the new Republican Senate candidates. She said that they would need to know who I was when they were picking their leader. It seemed so improbable, but I did heed her advice and called most of the new candidates.

Just before the election, Maralee and I attended a Christian conference. The speaker challenged us to be completely willing to do whatever the Lord had in mind for us. I remember praying and telling the Lord I would still serve in politics and that I was willing to go as high as He wanted me to go in politics.

I wanted my legacy as a legislator to simply be that I was a statesman, not just a politician. People get into politics for various reasons—some for fame, some for power, and some for service. I felt like serving in government was a calling, and for me, it was a sacrifice. I knew a higher position would require even more time away from my wife, children, friends, and extended family. I knew that the higher I went, the more misunderstood I would be, and the more attacks my family would be exposed to. So saying yes to whatever the Lord had in mind was a very solemn moment for me.

True to Maralee's strong, continuous impression, we did take the majority by one seat. In addition David Hann lost his own Senate election, which meant that Senate Republicans were without a leader.

Now I had the green light to pursue the leadership role, and on the first ballot among my Republican Senate peers, I was selected to be the new leader. I was of course elated, and my wife, Maralee, was vindicated.

As I retold her part in the story, I would say that Maralee told me a couple of times ahead of time that I was going to be leader. She often reminded me that I was only listening a couple of times and that she told me many more times than that. There is a lesson in that somewhere.

CHAPTER 5

JUSTIN, PRAY HARDER!

T HE 2016 ELECTION night started out poorly for us, with David
Hann projected to lose just after the polls closed. How could
we win a majority when we just lost our leader?

But as the evening progressed, we were holding our own. We
would win some; they would win some. It was going to be very
close. We were down to just a few districts left, and the balance of
power was yet undecided. Two of our candidates, Paul Anderson
and Justin Eichorn, were not expected to win, but their races were
within a hair.

Paul Anderson was running in a suburban district where Hillary
Clinton trounced Donald Trump, beating him by 9,375 votes. But
somehow Anderson beat the Democrat by 195 votes. That kind of
a difference is very rare, and Anderson's win reflected on his many
positive attributes.

PRAY HARDER

Justin Eichorn was not even going to run. Grand Rapids, in
north-central Minnesota, was an area served by Democrat legislators for generations, and Tom Saxhaug seemed unbeatable. Mike
Campbell had approached Justin in the spring about running for

the seat. No one was going to challenge Saxhaug. The filing deadline was in the early summer, and when it was just hours away from closing, Campbell called Eichorn one last time and asked him if he was going to run. Justin said he was praying about it. Campbell responded, "Pray harder!" So, at the final hour, Justin filed to run for Senate, not even thinking he would win. He ended up winning by a few hundred votes. Had Justin not tried, Senator Saxhaug would have run uncontested, and Democrats would have had the Senate majority.

Another candidate, Andrew Lang, defeated Lyle Koenen in the Willmar area. That district had been trending toward Republicans. At first several of us tried to get Koenen to switch to our side. His voting record aligned much closer to us. But in the end he could not do it. Lang was a veteran helicopter pilot and turned out to be a formidable opponent. He won too.

LEADERSHIP TRANSITION BEGINS WITH SONG OF PRAISE

I became the Senate majority leader. My peers voted for me. But I had no idea what I was getting myself into. As I went to bed that night, my head was swimming with thoughts of all that had to be done now that I was the leader. When I woke up the next morning, those thoughts were still there. The overwhelming magnitude of my new responsibilities was floating through my mind, and at the same time, as I was waking up, I was also hearing a beautiful worship song called "Oceans" in my thoughts. I felt God's pleasure in my taking on this responsibility. I didn't earn it, I had not been the leader, and I didn't work on the overall campaign to get us into the majority. I simply walked into the position.

That helped in our transition to the majority and treating the minority with respect and value. I had not been on the front lines of any messy, slimy ads or attacks. I didn't feel the need for vengeance or retribution, and that is not what our state needed either. Campaigns are often difficult, and the actions of the opposing side are often hard to forget. But when it's time to govern, all of that is best set aside, knowing that it will return in the next election cycle. But for now, I was willing to offer a clean slate to the Democrats in the Senate. That's not to say that I didn't have every intention of driving a conservative agenda, because I did. But I didn't have to be vindictive along the way.

I wanted the Senate to be the best it could be, and I wanted to create traditions within the Senate that aligned with its reputation of being a dignified body. Of course I wasn't going to be perfect in this regard, but as the twenty-ninth Senate majority leader since Minnesota statehood, I would do my best to point our body in the right direction.

There were many early decisions that had to be made as the new leader of the Senate. The first step was to build a leadership team.

BUILDING THE SENATE GOP TEAM BEGINS WITH MARALEE

When building the dominant Senate GOP team, the first part of my team was my wife, Maralee. The beautiful thing about a good marriage relationship to a godly partner is that you often get advice that can be very helpful, even divine. You just have to be open to it.

Maralee took her role seriously as my advisor and ambassador of sorts. We were husband and wife, but in politics, we were more. If we were going to be in the Twin Cities as a family, she decided she would engage at the Capitol.

She interacted with the Capitol Prayer Network and other Christian groups praying for all the folks on both sides of the aisle that were working at the Capitol complex. She wasn't afraid to visit members of the Senate and the House from both sides of the aisle— she loved people. Thoughts and prayers are important, but then you need to act. Maralee would pray with various groups, and then she would go meet the people around the Capitol complex.

As I mentioned already, two months before the election of November 2016, Maralee told me that she felt that we were going to take the majority back and that I was going to be the majority leader, and it came to pass. She was full of wisdom and insight.

She introduced prominent ministers to the Capitol and advised them on what it takes to be influential with individual legislators. Mike Smith, Morris Vaagenes, Dave Duell, Harold Eatmon, Gary and Kristi Graner and their Bethel ministry team, and others all benefited from her approach. Alongside me, she worked with people like Autumn Leva, lobbyist for Minnesota Family Council, to help her approach legislators in a way that would influence them rather than get a brick wall from them. When there was an important moral issue being debated on the Senate or House floor, she was invited on the floor or gallery to pray that God's will would be done on that issue.

Before I was majority leader, years earlier, she had been praying that the Senate would have a godly leader. At the time, she didn't think it was going to be me. But when I was sworn in as leader and she was sitting by my side, the Lord brought to her remembrance the heartfelt prayer she prayed many years earlier.

Many said she really showed them how to release the love of God at the Capitol. One of the main chaplains said she was really the chief chaplain.

She really moved at the Capitol like a butterfly, which seemingly floats around but actually is pollinating the flowers. Her role was important as she moved spontaneously from place to place. But the depth of what she accomplished was not always visible.

She helped make me a better leader. I often speak a factual answer without feeling the emotions of it. That works well in navigating through a project or decision, but it is not always best when working with people. Maralee helped me to see how my approach was impacting people around me. She helped me learn to respond in ways that seemed less cold. Politics is about relationships, and in this arena, people can be offended, and you may never know it.

Maralee is also a professional artist. At the time, she was just getting back into creating art. She painted two Brainerd Lakes landscape scenes, one of moonlight over Gull Lake and the other of fall reflections over a pond. Someone encouraged her to enter them into the Grandview Lodge wine label contest. The winner would get their work displayed on about three thousand bottles of wine sold at Grandview Lodge.

She tentatively submitted the paintings into the competition, and to her surprise, both of her paintings won. She had only put her initials on the paintings, so most people didn't know she was the winner. She did not want to win because I was the local legislator but rather because her art was that good.

Later Maralee felt that she would have an opening to give a painting to Governor Mark Dayton, but she had no idea how that would happen. Then, within a year, Dayton was scheduled to hold the Governor's Fishing Opener on Gull Lake. The event would be hosted by Grandview Lodge, the place where Maralee's paintings were displayed on wine labels and prints were sold in the store.

This was the event where she decided to give him one of her prints. On the morning of the fishing opener, in front of all the TV cameras, Maralee presented the governor one of her framed giclée prints. People could see that both Maralee and I had a genuine appreciation for Governor Dayton.

Once, near the end of a session, Maralee and I were asked to pray publicly for the governor at the Minnesota Prayer Breakfast. It was an honor and a bit strange as well. We were in the middle of the end of session conflict, but we prayed a genuine prayer of blessing over Governor Dayton in front of a large group of people. It certainly didn't hurt our end of session results.

We never shied away from praying for people at the Capitol, Democrats or Republicans. Some politicians pander to people of faith, knowing that making that connection can help them politically. But I think most people can see right through that. We just felt that when someone was really struggling, praying for them helped link them to the One who could help them navigate their pain, God Himself.

MARALEE'S PAINTING DISPLAYED AT THE CAPITOL

Many of Maralee's paintings were displayed prominently in my Senate majority suite at the Capitol. I intentionally made my office available for GOP senators to come and relax if I wasn't using the office. One time, a senator came in, not realizing Maralee was in the suite of offices too. As he reflected on the beauty of many of Maralee's paintings, she overheard him quietly breathe, "It is so peaceful in here." That was her goal. She created an atmosphere of peace in a very combative environment.

One time, she was painting a commissioned piece for Senator Michelle Benson—it was going to be a surprise wedding anniversary gift for her husband. Maralee would bring the work into my Capitol office suite and work on it when we were on long floor debates. As she painted, she prayed for Michelle and Craig's marriage. During one of those painting times, the minority leader, Tom Bakk, and I went into my office suite to discuss particular issues. As we entered the office, I started to say that Maralee would need to leave, but Tom interrupted, saying, "Let her stay. I like to see her painting." Tom's wife, Laura, also loved painting.

This was near the end of the session in 2019. As I was negotiating the final deal with Governor Tim Walz and Speaker Melissa Hortman, Maralee was painting. We cut the deal and decided to have a press conference in the governor's reception room.

I'm not sure why, but we decided to have our spouses join us in the back room. We ended up all going out of that back room into the governor's reception room, where the press was waiting for us. The media was packed into the room, ready to hear the announcement that we had cut the deal.

Maralee's hands were still full of paint. As we opened the door into the reception room, we were heading directly into the media scrum. We laughed about it later. Maralee was presented as she truly was, an incredibly beautiful artist, working behind the scenes in her own way, making the Capitol a better place to work and build relationships.

I eventually added her to the Capitol Arts Board, along with Fred Somers, an internationally acclaimed pastel artist. Both brought helpful insight to that board. Maralee was responsible for getting the Outdoor Artists of Minnesota to display their plein air art at the Capitol. Fred Somers decided not to display his work because he felt it might be perceived as favoritism because of his position on the art board, so I decided to display three of his pieces, along with Maralee's paintings, in my majority leader suite.

MY FIERCEST DEFENDER, MARALEE

Maralee has always been my fiercest defender. She is forceful but not domineering.

She even confronted an advocacy group that was telling lies about me and other GOP legislators to raise money, as she had reached her boiling point.

This same huckster showed up at a Republican dinner to agitate GOP legislators in attendance. Maralee made a beeline toward this man. As she was confronting him, he said, "I know you are pro-life, but your husband is not."

That was the last straw. Not prone to swear, she got in his face and said to him that he was full of b***s***! She then walked away, and she thought I would follow her. I would not have initially confronted him; he didn't deserve that attention. But in that moment, I felt as if I should speak a word into his future. I got about twelve inches from his face and in a low and firm tone said to him that he was meant for so much more…and left. Later he was removed from the event. After he left, several female GOP legislators thanked Maralee for standing up to this person.

On another occasion, Maralee confronted a parade goer who said as I was shaking his hand, I was peeing on his leg at the same time. She said, "Excuse me! My husband has sacrificed a lot to serve you, and that's what you say?" I think that was her last parade that year. Campaigning can be grueling, and it was definitely time for Maralee to take a break.

I love her passion. Occasionally it can put me in tough spots, but it always comes from a heart of gold.

TOGETHER WE REACHED OUT TO NEW GROUPS

When I chose to reach out to new groups to build bridges, Maralee would often come with me. We attended a few Log Cabin Republican events, and we would warmly greet their LGBTQ members. According to their group, about one-third of the gay community leans Republican and shares most of the GOP platform values. Even though some of our socially conservative positions were different than theirs, they knew we were genuinely warm toward them. As we built a warm relationship with them, we were able to openly talk about our differences. If you can build a good relationship, then there is a way you can talk about issues that deeply divide us.

DINNER WITH THE SOMALIS

We were invited to a Somali Ramadan dinner. Some of the Somali ladies flocked around Maralee, and she exuded warmth for them. The same thing happened at a Hmong dinner. At the Ramadan dinner I told the group of Muslims that Maralee and I were Christians and that the next day was our most holy day, Easter. I went on to say that we would normally be up north at our home already but came to their celebration first to show them that we honored them. They felt our genuine love for them, even though most of that group voted for Democrats.

Most of the new groups that we met with leaned Democrat. But we built new bridges by genuinely showing them love and honor, not based on political views but simply individual value. I realize that some politicians appear to be faking their warmth, but I believe most people see right through fake.

After we finished dinner, they insisted that I do a video interview, which was also carried live in Somalia. I did my best to show the warmth of America. It was the grace of God that gave Maralee and me the ability to love beyond our own opinions and political positions. As a result we had great favor with many new people.

MARALEE WAS INVOLVED IN MY CAMPAIGNS

Maralee was elbow deep in most of my campaigns, strategizing right alongside me. Often she would whisper in my ear a thoughtful response, and as I voiced it, people were amazed at the wisdom of it. It was her idea, but they thought it was mine.

President Harry Truman said, "It is amazing what you can accomplish if you do not care who gets the credit."[1] Legislators in general are high achievers who typically like credit, but if you combine that with humility, it truly is amazing what can be accomplished.

Maralee was not a legislator, but she did a lot behind the scenes. She was an important part of the Senate GOP team, and she deserves a lot of credit.

CHAPTER 6

STANDING WITH THE BULL ELEPHANTS

THE REPUBLICAN SENATE, or caucus, had been deeply divided in our first go-around in the majority after the 2010 election. During that time, with twenty-one new Republican senators and sixteen incumbent Republican senators, there were too many freshmen with an abundance of zeal but not a lot of experience navigating the governing process. We had a swagger we didn't deserve.

Some of us divided into two splinter groups behind the scenes, the conservatives and the moderates. That kind of struggle still plays out today in Republican politics countrywide. Today anyone who doesn't fit a person's view of what a Republican should look like is labeled by some a RINO, or Republican in name only. It's not helpful; it's divisive, and it makes the overall group much less affective.

BULL ELEPHANT PRINT

A house divided against itself cannot stand, and the 2011 Republican Senate majority was not working well as a team. I landed on the most conservative side of the caucus. We met secretly to determine how to move our agenda within the Republican Senate majority. I even acquired a signed antique print of a bull elephant and had who I perceived as the twelve most conservative senators sign the back of the print. Then I hung it up on my Senate office wall as a reminder to not back down. As we progressed through the 2011–2012 session, there were times that one side of the group of Republicans would take down a bill that was presented by someone on the other side of our own group. I can only imagine what it would have been like to lead our group at that time, and when you are blindsided by each other, your private caucus meetings after session are a sight to see. The entire bunch as a whole was an amazing group, but we allowed unhealthy division within our ranks.

Fast-forward to November 2016. I had been elected as the Senate majority leader, and I didn't want to lead a divided group. The truth is there are very few issues that divide a conservative Republican from a slightly more moderate Republican. Usually the senator's position is simply a reflection of the district that member represents. We only had a one-seat majority and could not afford serious internal divides.

If you are going to win a majority as Republicans in Minnesota, you can't make any mistakes. One of the keys to winning is selecting the most conservative candidate that can win. In other words, if a district is moderate, select a Republican candidate that is slightly more moderate. You can't move any agenda unless you are in the majority.

HONEST CONFESSION

It was time to bring the group together and tell the story of the signatures on the back of the bull elephant print. I brought the print down to our caucus meeting. I said that we could not afford to be divided or we would not have the impact any of us hoped to see. I then shared with the entire group, senators and staff, the story of the print and signatures on the back. I also confessed that I was a part of causing division in the Senate Republican group of 2011–2012. I said I planned to take a new course with our new team and that it started with me. Either we were thirty-four strong, or we would not succeed. I then asked each Republican senator and staff member to sign the back of my bull elephant print, signifying that we would function as one. Each Republican senator mattered, each voice needed to be heard, and each member and staff signed the back of the print.

This process of governing the Senate was going to require more time to get consensus, and respectful and open conversations about why each senator disagreed had to happen. But this process would be worth it in the end.

PICKING TWO DEPUTY LEADERS INSTEAD OF ONE

Another step to bring unity into our caucus was to appoint two deputy leaders from our group instead of one. Michelle Benson, a brilliant thinker, was on the conservative side of our group, and Jeremy Miller, a pragmatic negotiator, was on the slightly less conservative side of our group. Picking both sent a message to our caucus that all voices really did matter to me.

Senator Benson really loved numbers and facts in a wonkish way that I needed, and she played an important role in navigating thorny issues, especially in Health and Human Services. Senator Miller turned out to be very good at negotiating agreements with the Democrats who also held power. Jeremy also played a critical role in building up the campaign side of the Senate GOP. Both ended up serving our team very well.

Another important step was forming each committee and deciding who would lead them. Determining who would serve as committee chairs and who would be on the committees was a critical step in creating a functioning team.

In my mind, among the most important committees with the biggest financial budgets, impacting the taxpayer the most, were the Finance, Health and Human Services (HHS), Taxes, and K–12 Education Committees.

I always looked to who I thought would best serve in these areas, apart from any other identity politics. For the state of Minnesota, putting the best minds in the most important spots was what I looked for. So I appointed Michelle Benson to HHS, Roger Chamberlain to Taxes, Carla Nelson to K-12, and Julie Rosen to Finance.

I mention this because years later there was a complaint that I was not promoting someone related to a specific group. As I thought about it, I realized that I had appointed women to three of the four most important chairman positions without even thinking about identity politics.

SERVANT LEADERS

Senators have egos. When the time comes to pick senators as chairs and then put all the senators on committees, it can be very challenging. Inevitably some will feel slighted for not being picked to chair a certain committee or not being selected to serve on certain committees.

It's hard to find a place for everyone to shine. A few of the senators intentionally stepped into smaller roles because they knew it would help the Senate GOP function better. Two senators that stand out to me for doing this were Dave Senjem and Bruce Anderson.

Senjem gave up his opportunity to be Senate majority leader in favor of Amy Koch in 2011. Later he did end up being majority leader for a year. He also gave up his chair position over Capital Investments to help recruit a Democratic senator to our side. Both of these actions made a huge difference for our team.

Bruce Anderson had lots of seniority but never complained if he did not get the most prestigious spots. He chaired the Veterans Committee because he was passionate about taking care of our veterans. But even then, when he felt that Andrew Lang would benefit from being chair of Veterans, he stepped down and became the vice chair of that committee so that Andrew could develop. These two senators, Dave Senjem and Bruce Anderson, were the ultimate servant leaders.

Occasionally I tinkered with chair positions, but when done, it usually was because making changes solved secondary problems as well. Roger Chamberlain was clearly one of the more forceful senators on our team, and I moved him over to K–12 to combat the aggressive posturing of the teachers' union. I then moved Carla Nelson over to Taxes, which she considered a win for her as well.

PUTTING THE TEAM TOGETHER

As I mentioned, as you select chairs and members for each committee, you are never going to make everyone happy. I was grateful for the team of senators and staff that helped put the groups together. I did not want to be a dictator-like leader, and making many of these decisions as a team made sense.

I always felt that when a leader willfully gives away power, he becomes more powerful. With that in mind, I also gave each chair tremendous power to make decisions over their assigned responsibilities. I would only step in if they were stuck and could not break through in negotiations, and that did not happen often. This was contrary to the House at the time, where everything had to be run through leadership.

Mary Kiffmeyer, who had the distinguished honor of being Minnesota's secretary of state and also served in the House, was selected to serve as the chair of State Government, primarily because of her knowledge of election law. She governed like Margaret Thatcher, the Iron Lady. She was not afraid to confront people, even me, but she was always respectful.

BLIND SENATOR GIVES
DRIVING DIRECTIONS

Bill Ingebrigtsen was chair of the Environment Finance Committee and Torrey Westrom was chair of Agriculture. Both lived in central Minnesota and would usually drive to the Capitol together. On more than one occasion on their drive down to St. Paul, Torrey would tell Bill, "Turn here." Every time they shared that story in caucus, we would all laugh because Torrey is blind.

It was hard to believe Senator Westrom could navigate the Capitol complex as well as he did. Occasionally he was late, but he was always prepared for a floor debate and was a master of the facts. He was a very good orator. Occasionally he would complain about the Capitol complex not being ADA compliant, and when he brought something up, we addressed it as soon as we could.

Inge, or Senator Ingebrigtsen, was a sportsman like me. We constantly bantered about who caught the biggest fish or shot the largest buck. Even though I don't think I ever admitted it to him, his trophies were bigger than mine.

Dan Hall became chair of Local Government. But one of the things I appreciated most about Dan Hall, whose office was right next to me, was his constant laughter and pranks. A former college All-American hockey player, Dan constantly hid hockey pucks throughout my office. Laughter around the Capitol was good medicine for all of us.

Gary Dahms became the Commerce chair. This was a tough decision because Karin Housley also wanted this position. She was gracious and became our lead voice on senior issues, and she also advocated for reform of Minnesota's liquor laws.

Bill Weber didn't get a chairmanship in that year, but he added a wealth of wisdom to a myriad of issues. He hailed from southwest Minnesota, and his folksy way seemed unassuming, but if he sunk his teeth into an issue that he thought needed to be fixed, he was formidable.

Newer senators like Mike Goggin and Rich Draheim did not initially get chair positions either, but they quickly filled in gaps where their expertise was helpful on the Energy and Housing Committees.

I was interested in developing future leaders, and I knew, as some have said, none of us is smarter than all of us. I also made sure each freshman Republican legislator served on at least one conference committee so they would learn how to negotiate with the House.

Another important piece of building the Republican team was deciding who would sit next to me on the Senate floor during daily sessions. This person had to be good at debates, understand the history of bills over the years, and not say something stupid that the press would take hold of. For me, the easy choice was Senator Warren Limmer. Warren was one of the longest serving senators, which gave him unique perspective on many of the issues we were debating. Most issues seem to come up year after year, so knowing the ins and outs of earlier debates really mattered. Over the years, Senator Limmer had taken on some of the toughest issues, so I could trust his seasoned debating skills and knowledge. It helped to have someone next to me that shared my values and could help take the load off me during a hotly contested debate.

TERM LIMITS

Senator Warren Limmer is the reason I changed my position on term limits. In the beginning I was convinced that all legislators should only serve a few terms and then leave the Capitol. But as I worked with Warren, a legislator for more than thirty years, I realized that at least some legislators need to stick around awhile. Long-term legislators, on either side of the aisle, are the keepers of institutional knowledge. Why something was done a certain way gets lost over time, and it is helpful if someone remembers why. In addition, if all legislators leave after a short period of time, the ones that have the most experience are the staff and lobbyists. If they are the ones that know the most, then they are the ones that are leading, not the elected legislators.

I have found that even without term limits, most legislators cycle in and out of office in about ten years. Maybe there is a need for more discussion on this issue, especially at the federal level, but I now believe there are good reasons not to have blanket term limits.

GOP STAFF MEMBERS

Another part of the team that is often overlooked is the staff. I never thought a senator was more important than a staff member, especially if the senator implied that in a conversation with a staff member. Most senators, on both sides of the aisle, know how critical the staff member's role is in passing legislation that works.

Probably the least acknowledged staff member that did the most to keep the Senate GOP together was Maureen Watson, or Mo. She took care of most of the grunt work, getting meals, buying my plane tickets, reserving meeting spaces, etc. To some it seemed like insignificant assignments, but she helped make the Senate GOP a place where people felt they belonged. Another behind-the-scenes staff member was Dan Mickelberg, our top fiscal analyst. Whenever I needed data on just about any issue, it seemed like the information I wanted was at his fingertips. I looked smarter because of him.

There are too many other amazing staff to mention, but throughout the book, I will mention a few, starting with my chief of staff, Kevin Matzek. Kevin did an amazing job putting together a solid team of Senate Republican staffers. I only chose to weigh in on the choice of executive staff members, and I only wanted to choose from the top three candidates in each of those positions. I did not want to pick people for the executive team if Kevin and Senator Dahms, who oversaw personnel for senators, did not agree they were top-tier candidates.

During the process to pick my executive assistant, I wanted to pick a particular person who had applied and was interviewed but did not make it into the top three. I chose not to hire this person, even though I could have as leader, because they did not meet the standards of my team. It was painful for me to tell the person they didn't get the job, but it was a standard the team respected that I kept for the good of the Senate Republicans.

Maralee ended up helping me find both my executive assistant and my personal legislative assistant. She has an uncanny ability to miraculously find what I needed. I was looking for personal staffers who would reflect who I was. Matt Steele and Paul Hultgren ended up being those people that she didn't know at the time but somehow came into her orbit. Both had to make it into the top three qualified candidates, and both ended up being perfect for me. Over time, they moved on and were replaced by other qualified candidates, like Scott and Rachel.

In addition to being a second set of eyes for me, Kevin Matzek was the key player in helping to decide when issues would come the floor for a vote and how to prepare for any opposition we might get from the minority party. Kevin shared similar values to me but also recognized that not everyone we would be dealing with did. He was always prepared. We were building an organization, and if I was the framer, Kevin was the finisher. He implemented the direction and smoothed out the rough edges.

One lesson about Senate staff is that most are developing skills that will then serve them somewhere else, usually still connected to government. I often felt it was an honor to help someone develop and then watch them get a prestigious job somewhere else. Even that still helped my ability to govern, as they advocated for our ideals somewhere else. Mike Campbell coined the term the Gazelka Diaspora to reflect the many staffers that went on to serve as public policy professionals for many industries. Virtually all of them left with fond memories of the Senate GOP team, and that reflected well on what we were trying to accomplish in the Senate. Often the credit for the team goes to the leader, but as I mentioned, Kevin Matzek deserves the credit for most of those folks.

With the Senate Republican team in place, my focus shifted to making the Senate a place where relationships were built and the work for Minnesota got done.

Hiring a Chaplain

One of the leader's responsibilities is to select a chaplain of the Senate. I wanted to find someone who shared my beliefs but also respected the fact that senators and staff have diverse spiritual views. I was also looking for someone who could be appreciated on both sides of the aisle. Maralee and I talked about who that could be, and we both thought it should be Mike Smith of Redeeming Love Church in Maplewood. He was just a few minutes away, loved St. Paul, and genuinely loved all the people he encountered. He served exactly as I hoped he would.

CHAPLAIN MIKE SMITH INVITED TO THE STATE OF THE STATE BY DEMOCRATS

I tried not to show too much Republican favoritism toward Mike Smith because I wanted both sides to feel like they could reach out to him. So I thought it especially perfect when a State of the State speech came along, and he was invited by a Democrat. The State of the State speech from the governor takes place in the House chamber, and all legislators and a few friends are invited to attend. I had considered inviting Mike Smith to this event but chose not to. So, to my surprise, as I was sitting in my designated Senate majority leader seat, I looked over to the Democratic side of the chamber and saw Mike Smith sitting with the Democrats. He had not been officially invited, but as we were walking into the House chamber, Senator Nick Frentz saw Mike Smith, grabbed his arm, and brought him into the chamber. He was truly the chaplain of the entire Senate.

Pastor Mike is a Bible-believing follower of Jesus. He is sensitive to the moving of the Holy Spirit. But his greatest attribute is his love for people.

CHAPTER 7

TOM BAKK AND THE BRONZE TABLET

T HERE WAS A lot of work in front of us. We had only had the majority for two of the last forty-six years. Much of what was in place was done by the Democrats. The Capitol building had been remodeled, and the available leadership offices in the Capitol were now ready for us to move in. We had put together our team, but now it was time to govern. Governing was going to require cooperation from the Democrats. We could not start a floor session until we had thirty-four members of the Senate on the floor, which is all of the Republicans if the Democrat minority decided not to help.

Every floor vote would require every Republican senator to be present, or bills most likely would fail. Now, post COVID, remote voting is allowed, but at the time, that option was not available. Two different Republican senators had heart attacks during the yearly session, normally from January to May. Two senators had parents who died during the session. Occasionally a Republican senator was sick or had pressing personal business that meant they could not be available for an in-person vote. Navigating all that was extremely difficult, and having some sense of cooperation was critical.

I needed to build a solid relationship with Tom Bakk, the majority leader before me, who was now the minority leader. I wasn't sure how this was going to go because Tom was one of the most gifted politicians I knew. One of his decisions, building an office building for the Senate so more of the Capitol could be used by the executive branch and the public, ended up being part of his downfall. The Senate building ended up being campaign fodder, a waste of money at a price tag of over $300 million to complete, it was said. And yet all the senators now have a secure office location and a private, safe place to park. In addition the Capitol now serves more people than it did before. Time will assess his decision, but it was part of what cost him the majority.

Tom Bakk had done a lot of work overseeing the Capitol remodel project as well. His background prior to serving as a legislator was as a carpenter in the carpenters' union. His expertise came in handy when many of the decisions needed to be made to return the Capitol to its original glory. It was a massive project that required the legislature to find space outside the Capitol to do the people's business. The Senate ended up needing a one-day special session just after senators vacated the Capitol. We ended up using a State Office Building conference room for that special session. Once the one-day special session was over, I went over to the closed Capitol building and saw all the scaffolding constructed all the way up to the ceilings. There was no way we were going to hold any meetings in the Capitol for a while.

Later, by plan, we used the new Senate Office Building for one full session, about a half year of work. We all had to be flexible and move around a lot to make everything work. Senator Bakk had to orchestrate all of that. One final decision worth mentioning that Majority Leader Tom Bakk had to make was to determine what the Senate majority suite would look like in the Capitol and how it would function. He thought he would be moving into this suite when the session began in 2017. His name was already on the door, but he had yet to move in. He had planned to savor this moment as part of the fruit of his labor.

You can imagine the surprise and disappointment of Senator

Bakk when he discovered on a cold November night in 2016 that Democrats lost the Senate majority. He was no longer going to be the majority leader, and he would not be able to move into the leader's Capitol suite he designed.

I certainly did not want to rub it in. I tried to put myself in his shoes. I needed to be able to work with him. We only had a one seat majority, and navigating the Senate was going to be extremely difficult. Obviously I was thrilled that they no longer were in the majority, but that did not mean I should dishonor Senator Bakk.

So rather than look for ways to humiliate Bakk, I looked for ways to honor him. I was under no illusion that he wouldn't try as hard as he could to take back the majority, and with a one vote majority, that opportunity might present itself before the next election cycle. A senator could die or take another opportunity, and suddenly a special election could switch the power to the other side.

THE BRONZE TABLET

A year or so earlier, a few senators gathered behind the Senate chamber in the Senate retiring room. We were discussing how we could honor all the senators who had to put up with a comprehensive remodel of the Capitol. The retiring room is a beautiful, ornate sanctuary behind the Senate chamber where senators can go and not be bothered by lobbyists or even legislators from the House. Most of the time, no one else is allowed in the Senate retiring room but senators. Often during a long floor session, senators will go back to the retiring room to eat or simply get a break. In the retiring room, there are gigantic glass paneled doors that can be opened to walk out onto the scenic Senate balcony, where legislators take private phone calls and some legislators still smoke cigars. On each end of the retiring room is a fireplace, and above each fireplace is a place for a large bronze tablet. Above one fireplace is a bronze tablet with all the names of the senators that first served in the Capitol after it was first opened for business over one hundred years ago. Above the other fireplace, there was no bronze tablet, just a place for one.

As we gazed upon the tablet void space, Senator David Tomassoni said we really should put a bronze tablet up there of all the senators here today. Senator Tom Bakk agreed it was a good idea, but like the first ancient tablet, he said it should be all the new senators that were elected and came back after the Capitol was reopened. Like Tomassoni, I said that it really should be all the senators who were here during the remodel. It would honor all the legislators that had to work hard to make everything work while the Capitol was under construction. In the end it would be the majority leader's decision, so we would be doing it Tom Bakk's way.

But Bakk was not the new leader; instead, I would be making the decision about the new tablet. If we did the tablet the way Tom Bakk recommended, in addition to all the senators' names on the tablet, the majority leader's name would be on top and in much bigger font. My name would be on top of the tablet for the next one hundred plus years. I liked that idea. But the more I thought about it, the more I didn't feel right about it. I then thought I could share the top billing with Tom Bakk, but again, I did not feel right about it.

It really needed to go to Tom Bakk. He was the one who oversaw the important project to protect this historic treasure called the Minnesota State Capitol. So I approached Tom and said I really felt like we should list the people who were here during the remodel, not after. "If we do that, your name will be listed on top, and not mine. Are you OK with that?" Well, what do you know, he thought my idea was best after all.

I instructed Secretary of the Senate Cal Ludeman to put the tablet together. I wanted an inscription above it to read, "This tablet records the names of the members of the 89th Senate during the historic restoration of the Minnesota State Capitol. This was the only Senate in state history to convene in three different locations."

I didn't know for sure if that statement was true, so I appreciate that nonpartisan staffer Tom Bottern verified it for me. I guess you wouldn't want a tablet displayed for the next one hundred years that wasn't actually true.

And one more unique fun fact to know is that the tablet lists sixty-eight senators when there are only sixty-seven Senate districts. During the eighty-ninth Senate, Senator Branden Petersen resigned, and during a special election, Senator Jim Abeler replaced him. Both of their names are listed on the tablet for posterity, and now you know the rest of the story.

As I mentioned, I felt Senator Bakk should be honored for his work during the Capitol remodel. Part of my soul wanted that glory, but it didn't feel right. In the end, by honoring Senator Bakk, he honored me back in many ways. We were still adversaries but much more cooperative than adversaries tended to be in the Senate. It also helped that both of us were from northeast Minnesota, and both of us were Iron Rangers. That unique connection would matter more in the years to come.

CHAPTER 8

DO GOOD, LOVE MERCY, WALK HUMBLY

THE FIRST DAY of the January 2017 session was very memorable for me. I was sitting at the Senate majority desk on the Senate floor. I had never been in this place before. I was in charge and was responsible for determining the direction we would go. Each floor session, the majority leader works with the president of the Senate to orchestrate how the session on that day will go.

Each state is a little different. In some states the president of the Senate is the highest position, but in Minnesota, the Senate majority leader is the highest leader. It is confusing from the outside looking in because the president is perched high above the rest of the senators, running the meeting at the rostrum. The majority leader is running the meeting from his floor desk. This worked perfectly for me. I was leading, but often my work was behind the scenes.

As I sat at the majority leader desk on the Senate floor, I opened the center desk drawer and saw the signatures of some former majority leaders permanently scribbled onto the drawer. It was my turn now, and I did the same thing.

DO GOOD, LOVE MERCY, WALK
HUMBLY BEFORE GOD

On that first day of my leadership, I laid out my plan and direction for the Senate. As my goal was to lead the Senate in a way worthy of its reputation, I shared a personal treasured scripture with the entire body. I paraphrased Micah 6:8 and said, "This is how I want to lead, by following the principles of this scripture which says, 'And what does the Lord require of you but to do good, love mercy, and to walk humbly before him?'" My goal was to serve as leader of the Senate, doing good, loving mercy, and walking humbly. I shared this with the entire body and said that if they did not see me leading under these principles, to please point it out to me. I was genuine in my request.

That didn't mean I wasn't going to fight. I had every intention of driving a conservative agenda, but it could be done with Christian grace.

After that day, the Senate was now organized and up and running, and I was officially the new leader.

Just because we were now organized didn't mean everything would always go smoothly. Minority Leader Bakk still had to see if I was a pushover. To start the daily session, it required thirty-four yes votes on the Senate floor. So any time one of my members was missing for any reason, unless I had help from the Democrat side, we couldn't start the day.

One time, we were obviously short, and Senator Bakk was not in the mood to give me any extra votes. We went back to my majority leader suite, the office suite that just a few weeks earlier still had his name on it, and discussed the fact that I didn't have the votes. He asked what I was going to do about it.

I was not interested in trading anything for this. I basically said that if they didn't want to help do the people's business, I would simply hold a press conference and tell the media that I didn't have their support. I was already trying to create a fair arrangement for the minority party. I even made the makeup of the committees very

close regarding the number of Republican and Democratic senators serving on each committee. Making the Republican number of
senators on each committee one or two more than Democrats on
each committee meant more discussion and input would often be
needed from the Democrats on many bills. I wasn't about to budge
on starting the day-to-day meetings.

I was also tested by a few senators on my side as well. Once, a
high priority Republican issue was questioned by one of our powerful chairs. But the opposition to the issue was only said privately
to me. I was told I would not get this senator's vote on the bill if it
came to the floor. The day came that the tax bill, with this provision, was to be voted for on the floor. Again, the senator privately
told me they would not support the bill. I finally said, "I'm bringing
the bill to the floor. If you don't want to vote for it, then you will
have to explain to your constituents why you did not want a good
tax bill with lots of tax reductions." The vote came, and what do
you know, the senator voted for the bill.

DON'T BE AFRAID TO FAIL

As a leader, sometimes you must be willing to force the issue and
not be worried about whether you succeed. I might have failed in
that moment, but I didn't. I was never worried about looking bad. If
it was the right direction, I was willing to roll the dice.

SINGING PRAISE

I settled into my daily routine. On most days, my executive assistant, Matt Steele, organized a meeting with a different lobbyist
about every fifteen minutes throughout the day. It was exhausting,
and my voice was sore, but I was happy. I felt like I was in a good
groove for now. One day, as I exited our meeting room, Matt interrupted me and asked, "What does 'Do, do, do, do' mean?"

I asked him what he meant. He said that almost every time we
finished a meeting, I was humming those words. As I thought about
it, I was humming a worship song, but I'm not a great singer, so he

had no clue what tune it was. "Do, do, do, do" was "Shout to the Lord." I was enjoying the new role, and in my own way, thankful that God had put me here. Everything seemed to be going well. I wasn't afraid to tell people where I stood on issues, in favor or against, and I felt God's pleasure in me as I led the Senate this way.

Eventually the pace slowed a bit. I became more selective of the lobbyists I would see. I had Matt take some of the meetings himself, and I also had Matt direct more of the lobbyist meetings to the chairs that had oversight. This was a huge load off my plate and allowed me to focus on another one of my main responsibilities, fundraising for the caucus. In addition, when it was time to be involved with serious negotiations with the House and governor, I would not have time for meetings that others could handle just as well.

RAISING MONEY

One of the primary roles of being leader of the GOP Senate caucus was to raise money for the upcoming election. I was never involved on this side of Senate GOP before, but my sales background helped prepare me for the important task of raising money.

So while most of the legislators were almost completely focused on the session, I had the additional focus of raising money for the team. In prior elections we were outspent by the Democrats by more than four to one. I vowed to never let that happen again. The state Democratic party was a well-oiled money-making machine, but the state Republican party was in disarray and could not be counted on for financial help. It was up to us.

On the Senate legislative side, I would talk daily to my chief of staff, Kevin Matzek, about the legislative issues we were navigating. But at the same time, almost daily, I was talking to Mike Campbell on the political side about financial donors who might be interested in supporting our cause.

I did a lot of cold calling in my insurance business over the years, asking for a client's business. Now I was doing a lot of cold calling to ask for money for our caucus. Campbell would suggest I ask a certain client "for $25,000; that's what they gave last time." Instead, I would ask for $50,000. What's the difference? They can always say no, but some said yes.

You Win a Majority by Building Alliances

It wasn't until I was leader that I fully understood all the behind-the-scenes activities that must be navigated by the leader. I had to help our significant donors understand the alliances that I needed to build to win a majority. One successful business leader asked me why I needed to support all that pro-life stuff. I responded that if we did not have the pro-life voters, we would have never won the majority. If we didn't have the majority, we couldn't work on tax breaks that would benefit his business. Then the light bulb went on for him, and he understood the reason for alliances. Pro-life supporters needed to understand that we were building alliances with the business community. The business community needed to understand why I was reaching out to blue-collar unions, and so on.

Winning was about getting enough people to believe your team was the best choice to lead the state.

The House Is the House

The Senate was running well, but we also needed to work with the House, and they did things differently than the Senate. For a bill to get to the governor's desk, both the House and the Senate must pass an agreed upon bill with the exact same language in both bodies. In 2017, the first session I was leader, the House was also controlled by Republicans, with their leader, Speaker of the House Kurt Daudt.

You would think that because both bodies were controlled by Republicans, everything would magically get done and get to the governor's desk for passage of the bill or a veto. But that was not reality. Even when Democrats had complete control a few years earlier of the trifecta, they still fought as well. I can remember during that time that public comments were made by Governor Dayton about being stabbed in the back, etc., that spilled out into the ever-watching media.

Kurt Daudt had been the leader of the House for the last two years. He was politically savvy and always ready for a fight, and he was used to being the voice of the Republican opposition. As I mentioned, the House is much different from the Senate, and I was much different from Speaker Daudt. Governor Dayton and Speaker Daudt were constantly at each other's throats.

Their resentment of each other was impossible to hide, and it was causing unnecessary gridlock. There are times of warranted gridlock because two sides are diametrically opposed to each other's positions. But there are also times when personality and offense make a person always believe the worst of their adversary.

Create a Culture of Honor and Lower the Political Tone

When I took over the Senate, I aimed to lower the political tone at the Capitol. I intended to be diplomatically firm, but I would choose to be kind at the same time. In my marriage or in my business dealings, I never saw constant fighting and bickering as an effective way to accomplish anything good. So why would that be the best choice for governing?

There is a time for war, but it is not when you can have real peace and progress. The trick is discerning which season you are in.

Democratic Governor Dayton

In 2017 I wanted to try it my way. I chose to value Governor Dayton, even if I disagreed with him. I wanted the same in my relationship with Speaker Daudt too. I also took some early chances and chose to trust what Governor Dayton said, and he kept his word with me. A handshake deal proved to be true.

As we began to build an adversarial relationship on trust,

Governor Dayton was ready to give his first State of the State speech to a Republican-controlled House and Senate.

The State of the State events are filled with pomp and circumstance. The Senate enters the House chamber, with Senate leadership in front, to thunderous applause from their House counterparts. The supreme court justices attend, and the rest of the statewide elected leaders are there with other dignitaries as well.

DAYTON COLLAPSES

As everyone took their seats, the governor readied himself for his speech. On this occasion, January 23, 2017, things did not all go as planned. The governor had spoken for some time and had received rousing handclaps from legislators from his party and polite claps from the opposing side. Suddenly the atmosphere shifted. The governor started slurring his speech and wobbling. Soon his head crashed into the podium, and he crumpled to the floor. Those of us in the audience could not see him lying on the ground.

I immediately moved into action. Two of our senators, one from each party, were doctors. I motioned for Scott Jensen to come to Governor Dayton's side to offer help. Matt Klein also helped. The room was eerily quiet. The media tried to get around me for a shot of the governor sprawled out on the floor, and I would not let them by. One of the elected leaders from the opposing party saw me praying under my breath for our governor, came to my side, and settled under my arm as we continued to pray for Minnesota's governor. It was scary but ended up being less serious than it could have been. The governor was able to leave under his own strength, and we adjourned the State of the State meeting.

I bring this up because, unknown to me, the governor later watched the video replay of the events of that night. He saw how I protected his dignity. It wasn't fake. In the urgency of the moment, my actions were to help and defend Governor Dayton, regardless of our political differences.

We both felt that even though we often disagreed, we could trust each other's word. The goodwill was producing results in legislative roadblocks we had to solve, like the shortfall in dollars needed to keep private health care solvent. Even though Governor Dayton was pushing for public health care, he respected my concern for the private health insurance market and helped keep it solvent.

A GESTURE OF GOODWILL

One of Governor Dayton's commissioners, Katie Sieben of the Public Utilities Commission (PUC), was yet unconfirmed by the Senate. The Governor had privately requested a few weeks earlier that I confirm her. Often those types of requests can be traded for some personal request on my side. In this case I simply decided to schedule her for confirmation on the Senate floor one day and confirmed her.

I was buying goodwill, a commodity needed when you need to trust your opponent to do what they say they will do. Each positive decision made legislative agreements easier to get to.

Unfortunately Speaker Daudt was never able to build a trusting bond with the governor, or me for that matter, so it really was hard to get anything done. I ended up siding with Daudt on political positions but trusted the governor to follow through on our compromised positions, which he did.

I think if Kurt and I had got along better, we would have been more effective in our dual leadership roles, but that didn't happen. We both tried several times to meet and hash out differences, but we never united as leaders on the same team.

In the end I did lower the tone, and those around the Capitol noticed the change. It was easy to compliment other Republicans, but I was also not afraid to publicly compliment a Democrat, including the governor, if they did something right. There are plenty of times that you have to publicly correct the opposition, so if there is an opportunity to say something good, why not take that opportunity?

I know that most of the people of Minnesota appreciate when

they see genuine, cordial behavior from their elected officials. Some activists on both sides don't like it, but I believe most think it is a positive attribute in their political leaders.

RESPECTFUL COMMUNICATION

I asked my communication team to change their rhetoric in press releases penned for me. If a press release was particularly full of venom, I would ask them to reword it. There is a time to pick a fight, but it doesn't have to be every day. Bill Walsh, one of my key communication team members, began to intentionally put bombastic comments in press releases for me to agree to, waiting to see how long it would take for me to find it and weed it out. He would laugh when I pointed it out and tell his team that I would object. He called it the Gazelka way. And that's the way I wanted it.

CHAPTER 9

GOVERNOR DAYTON DEFUNDS THE LEGISLATIVE BRANCH

WORKING WITH TWO other headstrong leaders, Daudt and Dayton, was part of the territory. You don't get to be a leader by being a pushover. They each had their own leadership style, and together, it was not working.

In that year, I was considered the peacemaker. An opinion piece even used that term, hinting at the scriptural reference to it, Matthew 5:9.

The Senate GOP negotiating team consisted of me and Senators Julie Rosen and Jeremy Miller. Others, like Benson, Chamberlain, and Newman, would also engage, but Rosen and Miller were the core. Kevin Matzek, my chief of staff, played a critical role as well. Depending on the situation, Dan Dwight would engage also.

Matzek was rock solid in his role after the deals were made between the House, Senate, and governor. Many of the remaining details were worked out between the three chiefs of staff, and Kevin knew what he was doing.

Rosen, the Bad Axe

I was usually the good cop, so Rosen would be the bad cop. She had a way of getting under a couple of our opponents' skin...bad cop. Both Rosen and I were given the firefighters' Golden Axe Award. They wanted to show their appreciation for our legislative work related to their profession. As a result of that honorable gift, I was in the habit of calling Rosen the bad axe, instead of the more common term that would express her toughness.

For negotiations with the House and governor, I also wanted to create a team of decision-making chairs who would be involved in the actual decisions made and didn't have to look to me to solve their problems. They would become the problem solvers. This proved to be a very good strategy. There were a few times I would have done it differently, but the overall objective was worth a few mistakes. I gave credit for good decisions to the chair, and I took responsibility for the few bad decisions they made.

I had a long-term plan, and that was to only be in the Senate for a season, develop people to do the job, pass the baton, and move on.

Finally, most key parts of the negotiations were discussed privately with our entire GOP caucus. Occasionally they would push back on the direction negotiations were heading, and they were not afraid to say something. They made the whole process even better. If the disagreement was strong enough, we would take a different approach.

Prior Negotiations with Bakk and Daudt

For the prior two-year budget, Speaker Daudt worked with Majority Leader Bakk to work out a budget plan without including the governor much. After it was all settled, that story came out. The story circulated that Dayton couldn't get it done and Bakk and Daudt had to do it.

Governor Dayton did not trust Daudt or Bakk, and vice versa was just as true. My problem, as I mentioned earlier, was that I was stuck wanting to navigate like Governor Dayton but holding positions like Daudt.

Dayton also looked for compromise and someone that wasn't trying to pull the wool over his eyes. He wanted a handshake deal and to know your word to meant something. I think that's why we got along.

You can pull the wool over someone's eyes once but never again. As the saying goes, fool me once, shame on you; fool me twice, shame on me. I think the government works best when each side can call something a win. If one side is ridiculed, it's unlikely they will try to find agreement in the future. As we hashed out that first two-year budget in 2017, it looked like we were going to get to the finish line with a compromised budget we could all live with and agree on. The problem was the House Republicans did not trust the Democratic governor to keep his promises.

THE POISON PILL

The House Republicans wanted to slip a poison pill into the state government bill that said if the tax bill, which reduced taxes, was not signed by the governor, then in return, the Department of Revenue would not be funded...at all.

What made it more challenging for me is that the House Republicans wanted it to be a secret poison pill. Up to that time, everything was negotiated openly, fought for, and finally agreed upon. This was a complicated situation in that I too wanted the tax bill completed; it was the biggest Republican win. But, like the governor, I wanted everything above board. Unfortunately, unless the House and Senate agree, a bill never gets to the governor's desk to sign.

The House and Senate were at an impasse. Day after day we would lock horns. During this time, my daughter had a prom event at her school in Brooklyn Park. I was to give her a corsage before the event started, but I was trapped in negotiations with the House GOP. I knew we were not going to get anywhere with the House that day, so I told my team if we reached a certain hour, I was going to get up and hand negotiations over to Senator Rosen. The final deal was going to be cut by me, but I knew it was not going to happen then. Sure enough, the hour arrived. I simply got up and told the House negotiation team that we would keep negotiating, but Senator Julie Rosen and my team would handle it for the rest of the day. They were not happy, but I am so glad I did not miss out on that important event for my daughter. I knew nothing was going to get done that day anyway.

House and Senate GOP Can't Agree

The days clicked down to the end, and we needed to move things forward. I had no problem being stubborn on positions with the Democrats, but I was always surprised when I was at an impasse with the House Republicans. This was all behind the scenes, and if it spilled over publicly, it would make Republicans look bad. So I chose to accept the House strategy even though I did not agree with it. I was pretty sure I knew that the governor's response would be intense, and rightly so. House Republicans were sure he was going to veto the tax bill, and that is why they demanded the poison pill. I didn't think he would veto the bill because with several issues throughout the session he kept his word to me when he gave it. At the very minimum I wish I had argued for an open discussion of the poison pill with the governor, rather than sneaking it into a bill; that's on me.

That's not to say poison pills don't get into legislative bills; it has happened for centuries. But if you can do it a better way, you should choose the better way.

So as the final group of budget bills passed and got to the governor's desk, everything went smoothly…until he found the poison pill. As I expected, the governor was livid. Late that evening, Jaime Tincher, Dayton's chief of staff, called me up to ask if I knew the poison pill was in the bill. I responded regretfully and truthfully that I knew.

GOVERNOR DAYTON DEFUNDS THE LEGISLATIVE BRANCH

The governor then took his own course of action. He signed all the bills, including our tax bill, but at the same time, he line-item vetoed the legislative budget. There would be no money for the legislature.

He can't do that! But that's exactly what he did. We ended up before the Minnesota Supreme Court, debating whether the governor had a constitutional right to defund the legislative branch. I remember sitting there before the justices, thinking this all could have been avoided. The court didn't want to weigh in on this political fight. They ordered us, the governor and the legislative branch, into arbitration. We had to secure a prominent attorney. We wrestled with the issue for months and months, with dwindling money available for our expenses to run the legislative branch. I told the Senate Democrats that they would not receive less money than we did in the majority because of the governor's actions. I guess we could have said the minority staff were not going to get paid, but that would have just created another long-term problem. This fight needed to be shaped as a fight between the legislative branch and the executive branch, not a fight between Republicans and Democrats.

In the end we financially limped into the next year and moved forward during the next session. The court didn't rule one way or the other, but it was clear to me that the governor should not have that kind of power. The power of the purse belongs to the legislative branch, but certain actions of the legislative branch should be reserved for desperate times.

The following year was not much better. We were trying to put together a large bill that included many reforms that were objectionable to the governor. As the session was nearing the end and our bill, called Omnibus Prime, was ready to pass the House and the Senate, the governor sent us a letter outlining over one hundred items he would not accept in the final bill. Senator Julie Rosen was my Finance chair and as we talked together in the back of the Senate chamber, we were certain that the governor meant what he said—he would veto the bill. Keep in mind, there was no way I would have the votes to override any veto; we had a one-vote majority. Our Senate team assessed that the governor might take ten or twenty of our reform items but definitely not all one hundred that he marked as unacceptable.

Once again the House was sure the governor would cave in. Again we could not come to agreement with the House, and the days were ticking down to the required end of session. We ran out of time to negotiate with the House, let alone the governor. It was apparent the House was not going to bend, so I told our team to wrap up the bill as is and let it be sent to the governor. As we expected in the Senate, Governor Dayton followed through on his threat and vetoed the bill.

The House GOP publicly proclaimed that the governor was at fault, but not getting it done was a two-way street.

Most political experts agree that the governor usually gets more of what he wants than the legislative branch. In a divided government, if you get 50 percent or more of what you want, your base of supporters might not be happy, but you actually won. But in this case everyone got zero.

If there is no sense of respect or trust, what should get done doesn't get done, and everyone usually loses. That's what happened that year.

So why did I give into the House GOP position? The challenge was I did not think it was beneficial for the public to see Republican leaders from the House and Senate squabbling about the fact that we couldn't govern together. It was frustrating because my negotiation approach was more like finding a win-win scenario, and Kurt's style was more like finding a win-lose scenario. As a result we butted heads on a regular basis.

I like winning, but if the other side is required to leave the negotiation table humiliated, then future negotiations will be even harder.

#MeToo Movement in Minnesota

During late 2017 the #MeToo movement, a movement that encouraged victims of sexual assault to share their experiences, caught up with Minnesota.

Dozens of powerful men in politics, entertainment, and business had been sexually harassing women without consequences for years. With the rise of the #MeToo movement, that was finally changing.

In Minnesota's Senate, Democratic Senator Dan Schoen was accused of sexual harassment and was pressured by his leadership to resign, and he did in December of 2017.

In Minnesota's House, Republican Representative Tony Cornish was accused of sexual harassment and encouraged to resign by his own leadership, and he also resigned in December of 2017.

Senator Al Franken Resigns

US Senator Al Franken from Minnesota was also accused of sexual harassment, and because of immense public pressure, he officially resigned January 2, 2018.

This has been an important movement. Women in the workforce have had to endure repeated unwanted sexual advances from powerful men. Now those types of men need to think twice before they continue those unwelcomed advances.

With Franken resigning, Governor Dayton had to appoint a replacement to complete Franken's Senate term. But in a bizarre twist of events, Governor Dayton announced that his lieutenant governor, Tina Smith, would finish Senator Al Franken's term.

When a lieutenant governor in Minnesota vacates their office, by Minnesota Constitution, the president of the Senate automatically becomes the lieutenant governor. That meant that Republican Senator Michelle Fischbach was now designated to be the lieutenant governor. This provision rarely happens, and in this case, if Senator Fischbach could not also maintain her role as president of the Senate, the Senate would be tied 33–33. That would then require a special election, with the winner determining the majority for the Senate.

MORE LEGAL WRANGLING!

We, the Senate Republicans, argued that Senator Fischbach could keep her Senate seat while performing the role of lieutenant governor. We argued this because of an earlier precedent where someone served in both capacities at the same time. The opposing side, the Senate Democratic minority, argued that the constitution did automatically make her lieutenant governor, but as a result, she needed to resign her Senate seat.

The political wrangling lasted through the session, which ended in May, and on May 25, 2018, after the session concluded, Senator Fischbach resigned from the Senate and was sworn in as lieutenant governor. It was a unique situation. The political stakes were enormously high. If Senator Fischbach had stepped down from her Senate role early in the session, we would have been tied 33–33, and there would have been an early special election, with no other elections happening at that time. During special elections, fewer people are interested in the outcome. Special interest groups that would have loved to flip that seat have more influence when those elections don't line up with general elections. If somehow Democrats could have flipped that seat, they would have controlled the Senate for the next two years. The entire Senate was not up for reelection until November of 2020.

Picking Lieutenant Governor Smith to replace Franken was also tricky and risky for Governor Dayton. If for some reason he became incapacitated or died in office, Fischbach, a Republican, would automatically become governor. In 2018 Republicans controlled the House. If Fischbach became governor, and the Senate remained in Republican hands after a special election to replace her, Republicans would have the trifecta, House, Senate, and governor. We have never had all three, at the same time, in modern history.

I tried to make that case to Governor Dayton and the Senate Democrats. I proposed that we find an agreeable Senate Democrat to temporarily take the position of president of the Senate before Franken resigned. That would have created a smooth transition, with a Democratic senator assuming the role of lieutenant governor. But that idea was shot down. Democrats were rolling the dice.

GOVERNOR DAYTON INCAPACITATED

Then, in the fall of 2018, when Fischbach was the lieutenant governor, Governor Dayton had serious health issues. He was being treated at the Mayo Clinic in Rochester, Minnesota. He had back surgery on October 12 and 15, but due to complications, he was not released from the hospital until November 21, well over a month later. In my opinion, such a lengthy hospital stay means he was incapacitated, and we should have been notified. Fischbach should have assumed the role of governor for that time, and Republicans should have briefly had complete control, but we were never notified. Had it gone on much longer, we would have found out about it, and it would have created yet another constitutional crisis and battle.

Finally, the special election for Fischbach's Senate seat took place in November of 2018, Republican Jeff Howe kept the seat in Republican hands, and Republicans kept the majority in the Senate by one seat. Another big shift in the November election of 2018 was that House Republicans lost the majority.

The 2018 November election did not go well for Republicans in Minnesota. The House Republicans were removed from power, and a new Democratic governor, Tim Walz, was also elected. But by the grace of God, we kept the Senate Republican majority by winning the special election to replace Fischbach. It appeared that the one-seat majority was meant to be my lot in life as Senate leader.

Dayton served honorably as governor for eight years. He had to battle strong Republican leaders for six of his eight years as governor. He was part of the longest shutdown in Minnesota history in 2011. I wasn't leader until 2017, but we also had epic battles, some even leading to the Minnesota Supreme Court to sort them out. He had a temper that at times spilled over, but he was generally direct and said what he meant. He hated when people didn't honor their word or a handshake deal, and I feel the same. We were adversaries politically, but we remained friends after he left office. When our youngest graduated from Maranatha Christian Academy, Mark Dayton came to her graduation party and was warmly received by a host of Republicans. He loves Minnesota, and so do I. That's why, though difficult, we could make it work. Respect, honesty, and honor go a long way in making government work.

BEHIND THE VEIL WITH GOVERNOR TIM WALZ

Senate leader Gazelka and Governor Walz at a press conference at the beginning of COVID

Governor Walz and Senator Gazelka agree to a proposed budget May 19, 2019.

Governor Walz, House Speaker Hortman, and Senate
Majority Leader Gazelka at a press conference

Governor Walz shakes Senator Gazelka's hand after the initial agreement to lower
taxes during the 2019 budget negotiations. Speaker Hortman is on the left.

Three leaders publicly announce a budget agreement.

Three leaders sit down for the first interview with a Twin Cities reporter.

Three leaders smile for a photo after the first joint interview is finished.

A press conference signaling a budget agreement on May 22, 2017, with Governor Dayton, Senate Leader Gazelka, House Speaker Daudt, and minority leaders of the House and Senate

Senate Majority Leader Gazelka and Governor Dayton

Senate and House leaders and Governor Dayton

New leadership in the House and Senate

Governor Walz speaking to Senate Leader Gazelka

Gazelka rides with President Trump in the Beast.

Senate Leader Gazelka greets President Trump in Duluth, Minnesota.

Senator Gazelka and his wife, Maralee, greet President
Trump in Minneapolis. He has COVID-19.

Senators Chamberlain, Newman, Howe, and Anderson take a brief
break in the Senate retiring room behind the Senate Chambers.

Senator Gazelka and his wife, Maralee, prayed for Governor
Mark Dayton at the Minnesota Prayer Breakfast.

Senator Gazelka visits many police officers getting ready to stop the rioting in Minneapolis four days after the death of George Floyd.

Police surround the Minnesota Capitol to protect it from possible rioters after the death of George Floyd.

I N MY TIME as a legislator I served with three governors: Republican Tim Pawlenty and Democrats Mark Dayton and Tim Walz. I got along with all three governors, serving as the Senate leader against Mark Dayton and Tim Walz. But I had the most frustration with Tim Walz.

Socially I have enjoyed time with all of these governors at one point or another, and as I was originally writing the manuscript, I was generous in my thoughts about each one of them—but that was before Tim Walz was selected to be the vice-presidential candidate with presidential candidate Kamala Harris.

I had finished the basic manuscript in June of 2024, not even sure what I would do with the writing. But after I had completed most of it, American politics was turned upside down.

First, Trump's court wrangling came to a head with an initial guilty verdict to "Trumped up" charges. Then the US Supreme Court ruled that former presidents had quite a bit of immunity in regard to public acts as president.

Then President Biden had a spectacular flop in his debate against former President Trump. It was so bad that high profile Democrats and media favorites turned against President Biden, forcing him out of his bid for reelection.

If that weren't enough, a seemingly impossible-to-miss assassination attempt against Donald Trump failed. By the grace of God, the would-be assassin only nicked Donald Trump's ear instead of killing him, from only 130 yards away. It truly was a miracle he was not killed or seriously injured.

President Trump faced death that day, and instead of cowering, he forcefully rose up and encouraged the crowd to fight for their country. You never know what you will do in the face of fear or death, but Trump showed the country that he was fearless, an essential quality for our leaders. It was a very scary but inspirational moment.

Finally, as President Biden was knocked of his pedestal by former supporters, Vice President Kamala Harris took the reins as the Democratic candidate for president against Donald Trump. And whom did she pick as her VP running mate? It was Minnesota's governor, Tim Walz.

The importance of the chapters in my book about my dealings with Governor Tim Walz suddenly took on much more significance for the country. I couldn't simply be generous with my words about Tim Walz; I needed to be critical where that was warranted. Tim Walz was applying for the job to be the nation's second in command, and the people will decide whether Harris and Walz will get the job or whether it will be Trump and Vance.

I had direct internal working knowledge of Governor Walz. I was the one on the other side of the table as we negotiated two different two-year budgets. I was the one who worked with him and then against him during his use of emergency powers during the COVID-19 pandemic. I was the one who had internal private conversations during his lack of response to the riots destroying Minneapolis after the death of George Floyd. I'm the one who called the White House to get a message to Trump to intervene because Tim Walz was frozen with inaction after three days of rioting.

Then Governor Walz allowed the statue of Christopher Columbus on the Minnesota Capitol grounds to be torn down by a small mob who publicly announced their intentions the morning before they acted—and I spoke up.

After the riots subsided and Governor Walz continued to demonize the police by pushing anti-police legislation, I stood up and said no.

And finally, when Governor Walz would not give up emergency powers, I worked with the Democratic Speaker of the Minnesota House to remove his powers against his wishes.

So for the remainder of the book I want to focus on my time working with and then against Governor Tim Walz. I think looking behind the veil will help you see how he responded as a leader dealing with difficult challenges.

I do not believe Kamala Harris and Tim Walz should be given the reins of our country. Too much is at stake. Our enemies around the world don't care if our leaders are nice or not. They are measuring whether we are strong or weak, and that will be determined by our leaders. Neither Harris nor Walz has proven that they are good leaders; on the other hand, Trump has proven he is a strong, effective leader.

I do not think Tim Walz should be put in charge of our country as vice president. You be the judge.

CHAPTER 10

TIM WALZ BECOMES GOVERNOR

IN NOVEMBER OF 2018, with Dayton stepping down as governor in Minnesota, Republicans and Democrats battled for the executive office. The last time Republicans had won the governor's office was in 2006, when Tim Pawlenty was elected to his second term as governor.

Minnesota leans left, and unless the Republican candidate does everything right, he or she is bound to fail. After all, the last time a Republican presidential candidate won Minnesota was Richard Nixon in 1972.

In the end, as has been Minnesota's custom, Tim Walz handily beat Jeff Johnson to keep the governor's office under Democratic control.

Governor Walz was significantly different than Governor Dayton. He was much more comfortable out in the public eye. His country charm and folksy demeanor and dress did not fully reflect who he really was, a progressive liberal. He moved smoothly from group to group, with off-the-cuff humor that was endearing to those around him. He had been a teacher, a football coach, and then a congressman, and his communication skills would now benefit him as governor.

I had already been the Senate majority leader for two years, working through a tough negotiation period with Governor Dayton. Even though Dayton and I were political adversaries, we were respectful to each other and still remain friends today.

Governor Dayton preferred a handshake deal, and if he gave his word, he kept it. He hoped to have adversaries that would do the same. We got along well because we both negotiated in good faith.

Democratic Governor Dayton had controlled the executive branch for eight years, so the transition for Tim Walz to the position of governor would be easier than if the Republicans had controlled the executive branch and all the agencies it oversaw. Even so, Walz had to build his own team. He kept his congressional chief of staff, Chris Schmitter, and built his network from there.

The Republican Senate, under my leadership, was still in charge, and other than a few tweaks over committee assignments and chairs, we were ready to go. Governor Walz had to pick agency commissioners and a host of other folks to fill leadership roles in his administration.

Governor Walz was new and full of dreams of what he could accomplish. He thought, because he won the governorship, that he had a mandate for change—his change. He initially forgot that my Senate GOP team kept the Senate majority, and we didn't agree with his assessment that he had a mandate.

That's the nature of divided government. First it's divided into federal and state. But then power is divided within each state with that state's own executive branch, legislative branch, and judicial branch. Finally, if two parties share power, it is divided even further. That was the case under the beginning leadership of Governor Walz. He didn't know it yet, but he was about to find out how much power the Republican-controlled Senate really had.

Checks and balances are part of the original intent of our government design, and at times it can be very frustrating to govern within that system, but it is important. It forces people representing different perspectives to work together to find solutions that work for all the people they serve. And in this case it worked for all of Minnesota.

WALZ APPOINTS SENATOR LOUREY AS HUMAN SERVICES COMMISSIONER

One of Governor Walz's early decisions was to appoint Senator Tony Lourey to become Commissioner of Human Services, or HS. Walz was advised by Senator Tom Bakk, the Democratic majority leader before me, that he should not pick Lourey for the position because it could give Republicans another win in the Senate. But Governor Walz ignored his warning.

An appointment of a legislator to a commissioner position means that legislator automatically loses his legislative seat, and a special election will be needed to fill the vacant seat. Lourey's vacated seat gave Republican's an opportunity to expand our one-seat majority— and we did.

Our campaign team was getting really good at winning. We won the Senate majority in 2016, and we won the special election to replace Senator Fischbach. Now we had the opportunity to take an extra seat in the Senate.

For the special election we recruited State Representative Jason Rarick to run for the Senate. His blue-collar union background was a good fit for the district that included Cloquet and other northern towns. Cloquet had not been represented by a Republican in what seemed like a millennium.

After Democrats selected Tony Lourey's son to run as the Democratic candidate, we went to work identifying his strengths and weaknesses. We felt he was vulnerable.

We used new technologies, at the time, to laser focus on getting the right voters out and enhancing the Democratic opponent's negatives. We did that with late-night-TV-style humor.

If you ever want to run for office, you must think about what you post on social media. It is part of who you will be recognized as. We simply reposted some of the silly posts our opponent had posted himself.

We also organized new political friends to help us win. As leader I made a strong effort to reach out to the blue-collar unions. Long considered Democratic strongholds, blue-collar unions were being marginalized now by the Democratic Party. Many of their industries—like mining, energy, and manufacturing—were under attack by the Left. I made the case to blue-collar leaders, like Jason George of the 49ers (International Union of Operating Engineers Local 49), that we needed to forge stronger alliances. The blue-collar unions needed to work with the business community to fight together for the jobs in the industries I just mentioned. When Democrats delayed mining projects in northeast Minnesota, United Steelworkers was frustrated. When an oil pipeline working its way through the same region was constantly delayed by Democratic initiatives, 49ers and Pipefitters were agitated. Both of these anti-blue-collar-union initiatives continued under Governor Walz.

I decided that if Republicans were going to win in Minnesota, we needed more people on our side. One of my jobs after high school was working at Minntac, an iron ore mine in northeast Minnesota. I didn't mind the hard work, and the pay was great. My own blue-collar experience was positively received by union members. Blue-collar union workers have leaned toward the Democratic side for generations. But over the last few decades, their views on many hotbed issues began to align more with Republican positions.

However, the issues of right to work and prevailing wage kept them generally aligned on the Democratic side. But that was changing. I decided early in my leadership that I would never negatively change those private union issues in law if the blue-collar workers would simply join us. I started attending their gatherings and publicly shared my positions. I kept my word, and many blue-collar workers came our way. A couple of years later, Trump did the same thing in his run for presidency, and it helped him as well.

What I did expect from the blue-collar unions was that they work with the business community to fight together to keep their jobs here in America. I wasn't choosing sides; I was telling them that they both benefited from working together when Democrats no longer seemed to care about some of their industries.

I don't get the credit for the idea of aligning with some of the blue-collar unions. The Republican minority leader of the Senate before me, David Hann, gets the credit for starting this process. I just jumped in hard after the ball had started rolling.

As a result of this political shift, we got support from some of the blue-collar unions in the special election in District 11 that included Cloquet, Minnesota. In addition we had fantastic coordination from many groups that we already aligned with that hoped we would win, and in the end, we did win.

That win was a huge loss for Governor Walz, and it gave me real breathing room in the Senate. Now our majority was 35–32, which meant that if someone were missing for any reason, we could still function. It was still a lot of pressure, but it was amazing how much better it felt psychologically.

GOVERNOR WALZ REJECTS MY ADVICE

In Minnesota the Senate approves or rejects the governor's commissioner selections, so it would have been wise for him to listen to my perspective before choosing candidates, but he didn't listen. One example is the choice for commissioner of commerce, which in Tim Walz's administration also included oversight of energy issues.

Two Democrat lobbyists that supported Walz for governor were Paul Cassidy and Jason George. Cassidy represented insurance issues, and George was the head of the 49ers union. I respected both of these people and their positions. I told the governor that if both of them approved of his choice for commerce commissioner, I would support that person as well.

Sure enough, neither of his supporters supported the selection he made for commerce. It turned out that the person selected did a terrible job, and later, I had to remove him. I wasn't demanding. I was seeking reasonable compromises that we both could live with. But that was not the route he chose.

CHAPTER 11

NEGOTIATING THE BUDGET WITH GOVERNOR TIM WALZ

GOVERNOR WALZ WAS sworn into office in January of 2019. He thought he came in with a mandate, but being the leader of the executive branch does not mean you get to do everything you want without the support of both houses of the legislative branch.

In the House, Democrat Melissa Hortman became the Speaker of the House. Melissa and I both started in the House in 2005. She was clearly unashamedly liberal and, from that vantage point, loved Minnesota. She was also a lot more pragmatic than I expected her to be.

The Senate majority in 2017, under my leadership, was the lone Republican voice in Minnesota politics. All statewide elected officials were Democrat, and the Minnesota Supreme Court leaned heavily Democratic. We were Minnesota's last hope of stopping complete Democratic domination. Even so, it actually felt easier to negotiate against two Democratic opponents, Governor Walz and Speaker Hortman, than it did negotiating with a House GOP Speaker and a Democratic governor.

Both Governor Walz and Speaker Hortman were new to their

roles. Neither of them had ever had to negotiate a massive state budget. In addition, in comparison to my Senate GOP team, their teams were still green with inexperience.

I knew the ropes, but I wasn't sure how the two other players, Walz and Hortman, were going to play. In the prior two-year budget agreements, Dayton and Daudt were the other two players. First I had to get agreement with Speaker Daudt, which had proved difficult. Then we had to get agreement with Governor Dayton, which was also difficult. With the new alignment of power, Hortman and Walz both had to get agreement with me.

Governor Walz had a grand progressive vision of where he thought Minnesota should go, and it would require significant tax increases to fulfill. Minnesota was already a high-tax state, and I was not interested in raising taxes even more.

But he also wanted to solve problems. One problem that had not been solved and was left over from the previous few years was MNLARS, the Minnesota Licensing and Registration System. This program was tasked with modernizing the licensing and registration system in Minnesota. For years Republicans had argued that the direction Governor Dayton and the Democrats had chosen for updating this system, fixing it themselves, was not working.

The State of Minnesota had already spent over $100 million to update the system, and it wasn't even close to working. We recommended a third-party expert independently review the system and determine if we were heading in the right direction. Senator Scott Newman was relentless in his push in this direction, but Governor Dayton would not give in.

When Governor Walz heard the complaint from Senator Newman and me, he agreed that an independent, third-party review made sense. That agreement showed real promise for future negotiations.

Both sides agreed to have Rick King from Thomson Reuters dig into this problem. In the end, he determined that it was a broken system and needed a solution outside of Minnesota's IT Department. The new direction for MNLARS worked, and it pointed to promising outcomes in Minnesota's divided government with a new governor at the helm who was willing to accept at least one good idea from Republicans.

THE LITTLE BLACK BOOK OF SECRETS

As we plotted out our positions in January of 2017, I thought about what I thought the end of session in May would look like. As leader I carried a little black book for notes of conversations, goals to accomplish, offers to make, offers made by the other side, and comments I heard the other side make that might be helpful to remember later. In January, as the session began, I wrote down in that book what I thought the end of session deal should look like. For me, this was also a prayerful time. I regularly asked God for wisdom to find the right path for Minnesota. This was not just in how to treat people in the process but also what policies would be best.

The governor wanted to increase taxes to fund his progressive dreams. My goal was to have some tax decreases and no grand progressive dream. Other than tax decreases, I did not expect that the end of session would include any major conservative positions and definitely no major liberal positions. We certainly were going to pass legislation in the Senate to reflect our conservative positions, but I knew that in the end, the House and governor would be opposed.

The leverage I had was the fact that if we did nothing about the tax structure, the 2 percent provider tax, or sick tax, was going to sunset, or go away, at the end of the year. This tax was included on most medical and dental procedures across the state.

I was happy to let it go away, but rural hospitals said it would be devastating to them if that tax went away. Rural hospitals provide access to medical care in many remote places across Minnesota. If they are not profitable and have to close, that reduces access to medical care in rural Minnesota. So, with that in mind, I was willing to be flexible with the provider tax if the tax bill was an actual reduction in overall taxes. The provider tax was going to be the piece that I planned to give a bit on as the session squeezed to the end a few months down the road. But that was a closely held secret at the time.

As Minnesota's tax burden has risen to one of the highest in the nation, I tried to focus on reducing taxes that were the pressure points driving folks out of Minnesota—taxes on military pensions, taxes on Social Security, and taxes and excessive regulations on businesses.

If I was going to agree to not completely remove the sick tax, then in return, I was going to push for other tax decreases. I had already helped to get rid of the tax on military pensions, which helped encourage veterans to retire to our state. The next step was to work on getting rid of the tax on Social Security and the excessive property taxes on businesses.

That was my game plan from the beginning. I shared it with Mike Campbell, my Senate GOP political director. By having a clear sense of where I wanted to finish, when the opportunity showed itself in intense negotiations that would inevitably come, I would know it was time to cut the deal.

If you don't know where you are heading in negotiations, you won't ever be able to pull the trigger and cut a deal when you see it. In a divided government, where both parties share power, you must see what can be, not just what you want it to be. The final agreement is not going to be what you really wanted, but rather, something less. If you negotiated and got 55 percent of what you wanted, and the other side got 45 percent, you won. If you got more than 60 percent, you did really well.

CIVICS 101

That's the part that is hard for activist supporters to understand. In the end, neither side gets what they really want, and both sides are not completely happy with the outcome. That's civics 101—compromise where you can, and hold firm where you can't compromise.

As the session started in January of 2017, the Democrat-controlled House began passing liberal-leaning bills, and the Republican-controlled Senate began passing conservative-leaning bills.

The governor released what he thought the budget outcome should look like. One of several taxes the governor wanted to raise was the gas tax. But from the very beginning of the session in January, I said we would not increase the gas tax, or any tax for that matter. Republicans, rather than raising the gas tax for road projects, were adding more transportation bonding bills to the mix. We acknowledged that more money needed to be put into roads and bridges, but we didn't need more taxes to do it. In addition, with the rise of electric vehicles that don't use gas, more and more vehicles would not be contributing to the gas tax.

I never changed that position, and when I said something publicly, I did everything in my power to keep that position. I was careful in what I said publicly. I wanted my comments to mean something. When I said it, I did it. I wanted to make sure people knew I was a man of my word so they didn't have to wonder if I meant what I said.

What I never said publicly was that I planned to let the 2 percent sick tax go away. I was silent on this issue. I knew that sooner or later they would start to explore this issue, and I simply had to wait for them to get to that issue. I said no a lot to other tax increase ideas.

The second thing I looked for was the carrot my opposition really wanted that I could live with. I also had to discern who was going to be the driving force behind the direction we would go in negotiations. Was it going to be Speaker Hortman or Governor Walz driving the Democratic direction?

In that two-year budget cycle, it was definitely Governor Walz. So I paid particular attention to what he really wanted, and that was more funding for public education.

Both sides believe in funding education, but Republicans are not afraid to push for more reforms if the status quo is not working. Democrats are beholden to the teachers' union, and they simply, and always, wanted more money.

My give was going to be more money for public education than I thought was necessary. But in return I would insist on real tax reductions. Our education team, at that time led by Senator Nelson, would be pushing for reforms as well, and I hoped we would get some, but that would be up to her to get.

The wrangling, posturing, and public comments continued all session long. The bills passed in the Senate and House, and many were sitting in Conference Committees to be worked out. The Conference Committees include members from both the Senate and the House. It is their job to agree on a final bill that both bodies will support, and then send it to the governor to either sign into law or veto.

But nothing can be moved until there is an agreement from the Senate, House, and governor's office as to how much money we will allocate to each area. These are called the targets.

This was Tim Walz's first go-around. He positioned himself elbow deep in virtually all the main bills. Normally the House and Senate work to reach an agreement, and the governor's commissioners give input on what the governor wants to see.

This time was different. Because I had already been through this once, I decided that if the governor wanted to be hands on, I would lean into that. I felt like his decision to negotiate that way was to our advantage. All of my chairs were seasoned in negotiations, and all would help bring additional insight. Where I had given my chairs tremendous power to negotiate, the governor's commissioners had very little say in the final outcome. We had the upper hand.

The big sticking point was whether to raise taxes. The moment finally came when the governor finally gave up on all tax increases, and we began to discuss whether we should keep the sick tax.

3D CHESS OR CRIBBAGE?

I felt like the governor and his team were playing 3D chess, a normal feeling throughout every negotiation, but I was just playing cribbage. In cribbage you have 120 pegs to the finish line. It's linear. If I hadn't known where I wanted to end up, cribbage would have been the wrong approach, but as it happened, it worked perfectly.

I was sure of the moment and ready to negotiate the sick tax reduction instead of eliminating it for other tax reductions. But I had not shared that strategy privately with very many people. More than one GOP senator thought I was pursuing the wrong direction, and I felt pressure from them to change course. But I knew we were at the turning point in the negotiations.

I was finally at the place I was waiting for. The governor proposed that we leave the 2 percent sick tax in place. I countered that I was willing to reduce it, instead of the planned elimination of the tax. But in exchange I wanted a middle-class income tax cut, agriculture and small business property tax cuts, and a reduction in the tax on Social Security.

The governor's attorney, Karl Procaccini, said it was unconstitutional to cut the sick tax. He said we either had to eliminate it or leave it at 2 percent.

This was a sticking point I had not expected. I did not want to leave the sick tax at 2 percent. I wanted to lower it. Even though rural hospitals wanted the sick tax to remain, I knew that some folks would be upset if we did not remove it, so I wanted to be able to at least lower it.

This roadblock continued as we were spiraling to the end of the session. The pressure was building to reach targets for spending and tax reductions. Once targets are reached by the governor, Speaker of the House, and Senate majority leader, then the work of closing out bills can be done.

I was so grateful for the negotiating team I had around me. One final key player for the Senate was Eric Nauman, the nonpartisan principal fiscal analyst for the Minnesota Senate. Senator Rosen, chair of the Finance Committee, had worked extensively with Nauman and said she thought we should bring him into the inner circle. He had been hired long ago by a Democratic majority, so at first, I was wary of him. But he proved over and over again that he was interested in fighting for the interests of the Senate.

We were about to have another closed-door session with the governor. In these meetings, just a few people are present from each side. We usually did them in the governor's suite of offices. We knew that behind the meeting room doors, the governor had a host of experts ready to answer any of his questions. We would have to walk back to our offices to get advice from a much smaller group of experts.

We were coming to the end, and a deal needed to be cut. Just before what looked like would be a meeting to cut a deal, one of our leadership team, Dan Dwight, vaguely remembered a time that the sick tax was lowered to 1.5 percent. If that were true, the governor's attorney was wrong, and the tax could be lowered. Sure enough, we found out that the tax had been lowered around 2003. We printed that piece of information and went to the negotiation table, knowing we had a powerful card to play.

CHECKMATE ON GOVERNOR WALZ

As we sat down, we restated our positions, and the tax reductions we wanted. They were willing to give us some tax reductions, but only if we left the 2 percent tax in place because it "couldn't be lowered." They also wanted more money for education.

I think they thought they had us in checkmate. Then I slid the paper across the desk to Governor Walz, showing that the sick tax could be lowered. I said that if they felt like the law wouldn't allow us to lower it to 1.8 percent, then we would accept the even lower reduction of 1.5 percent that it had been lowered to in the past.

It was checkmate but on them. The governor and his team left the table and met privately for a bit of time. In the end, they came back and offered to accept our target proposals and the tax reductions I proposed, lowering the sick tax to 1.8 percent, if in return, I would accept funding education at the governor's position. We had already agreed to most of the other spending provisions. This was an important moment. Nothing was in writing yet. I could choose to go back to my team with the governor's offer or accept it. Rather than go back to the Senate suite of offices to discuss the proposal with our larger group, which is a good idea, our small team met briefly, and I decided to take the deal. This was the deal I was looking for, and now it was before us. I didn't want the governor to change his mind.

The deal was made, and a handshake and a signed agreement were executed. We held a joint press conference afterward, and all of us were happy it was done. We each got wins, which is important in government negotiations. We were all happy there was light at the end of the tunnel to finish the session on time.

You would think that would be the end of it, but like normal, getting a Democratic House and Republican Senate to agree on all the language of the final bills proved difficult.

This is where the legislative leaders have to help their chairs, regardless of party, get over the finish line. There are times that the chair just can't make the compromise needed to finish. In the heat of the battle, many chairs will not budge from their position. You do want chairs that are stubborn and fight for their position, because in the end, both sides have no choice but to give a little to get to a compromise. Some chairs simply cannot do that, and that's when the legislative leader must step in. The leader has to push and sometimes step on some toes and bruise some egos to finish the job. It's not easy, and sometimes those actions are not forgotten easily by the chair involved.

In 2017 Roger Chamberlain, the Tax chair, felt bad we didn't get more. Yet everyone around the Capitol saw his tax bill as a big win for Republicans. We had not had a middle-class income tax reduction in decades. Farmers, lower-income seniors, and small business owners all saw tax reductions as well. It was a big win, but in the heat of the battle, sometimes it doesn't seem like it.

Another impasse was the language in the Jobs Committee bill on wage theft. I was looking to toughen up our laws on wage theft, but I didn't want to go too far. It was a way I could show my support to my new blue-collar union friends. Eric Pratt was the chair of this committee and a good problem solver. I asked him to find some language we could all live with. In this area the governor let DEED (Department of Employment and Economic Development)

Commissioner Steve Grove do the negotiating. Pratt had a tough assignment; Grove was good at negotiating. The pressure was immense, the end of the session was looming, and on this issue, I felt we went just a bit too far. I wanted adjustments to the wage theft issue, but Grove got more than I wanted to give—only because I pressured Pratt to get it done. We tried to correct the mistakes the next year, but we did not get the cooperation from the Democrats we wanted. That was on me.

That pressure was always there when compromise was required to get a budget done and two ways to do it. That's how it always goes as you tumble to the end of the session.

In the end those around the Minnesota Capitol felt like Republicans won the session negotiations in 2017. But I knew that it was important not to humiliate my opponent. I called the session a draw.

The governor could declare a win, with more money for education. The Republican Senate could declare a big win by getting significant tax reductions.

As the sound bites came out, we, the Republican-controlled Senate, also took credit for large education funding increases, and Governor Walz and Speaker Hortman, Democrats, also took credit for all the tax decreases—that's politics.

The first two-year budget negotiations with Governor Walz and his administration felt like we got more than 60 percent, a real win. The next two-year budget, in 2021, was going to be much different. Both Governor Walz and Speaker Hortman were now seasoned leaders, and both now had teams that learned what it's like to be in charge.

CAMELOT

That moment, knowing we did really well in negotiations against Democrats controlling both the governor's office and the House, felt very satisfying. I called it Camelot because everything seemed to be going right. The Senate GOP was a close-knit team. I was the leader, but I was among many leaders that all had a seat at the round table. Almost everyone felt comfortable on our team. I did not rule by fear but rather by love and respect. We focused on what we thought was best for Minnesota. I probably heard one hundred times in the first three years as leader, from lobbyists and others watching the proceedings, that the Republican senators were considered the adults in the room.

As a group we were thoughtful, reasoned, and willing to negotiate in good faith to find solutions that all of Minnesota could be proud of. I never lost my cool, and that was true of most of my leaders, most of the time.

I didn't have any serious challenges from rivals in the Senate GOP. We often ate out together after the daily session at Burger Moe's in downtown St. Paul. They eventually gave us a back room with a very long table that we could all sit at. It wasn't just the GOP senators; our staff were welcome too. We even let GOP House members join us if they wanted to. Our political director, Mike Campbell, was always welcome too. We were working hard but having fun too.

Senators Having Too Much Fun

One time, one of our senators found a good deal on used go-carts and bought a few. He brought them to the private underground parking area of the Senate Office Building. The parking area is circular around elevators in the middle. You guessed it—they were racing the go-carts around the circle. I didn't hear about it right away. I'm sure they thought I would put the kibosh on it, but I didn't. However, I chose not to race. I decided, as majority leader of the Senate, that it might not be best to be in a picture of senators riding go-carts around the parking lot while we were negotiating with the governor and Speaker of the House.

Those were the days.

CHAPTER 12

SPEAKER HORTMAN AND FISHING WITH THE GOVERNOR

I was unsure how Speaker Hortman was going to be to work with. We started in the House together back in 2005. She was unashamedly liberal. Her role as leader first began tentatively, letting Governor Walz drive the bus. But by 2018 she clearly was carving out her role as leader of the House.

FINDING COMMON GROUND

When government is divided among Republicans and Democrats, learning to be pragmatic is important. It doesn't matter whether you are conservative or liberal in this regard. You have to be able to find the middle ground for the final compromised budget. Speaker Hortman, a liberal, turned out to be pragmatic. She would fight for liberal positions, as I would fight for conservative positions. But in the end, we both understood where the other person was not going to budge.

That understanding came from months of haggling, honest private discussions, and looming deadlines to pass agreed-upon bills. This process would unfold each session that we were pitted against each other. Special interest groups and activists from both sides would push us to support one side or the other of an issue. Eventually, if we were going to pass anything, we would have to compromise.

For some issues, like guns or abortion, there was very little interest on either side for compromise. Each year, each side would stake out their position, and each year, a bill representing that position would die.

Sometimes a package of tough issues would be proposed in private. For example, I asked if she would accept a bill requiring a photo ID to vote if I would accept some form of driver's license for immigrants here illegally. Both issues were controversial, and both would create a win and a loss for each side. If it actually were going to happen, it would then become public. But because we never got any agreement from each other on those two issues, they never were discussed in public as a possibility.

This is the kind of political relationship that serves the citizens best—two opposing leaders that respect each other, are pragmatic, and know how to find compromise in the end. On my part, I was slow to attack any of the opposing leaders I was up against, Governors Dayton and Walz or Speaker Hortman. This was especially true when we were close to an agreement. That is not the time to drop a bomb.

My public comments were about differences on issues. If I needed to take a shot at my opponents, I usually tried to make it more generic: "Democrat leadership says..." rather than "Tim Walz says..." If I was going to hit harder, I often called them privately to let them know what was coming. The goal was to keep a warm enough relationship to be able to hash out a compromise at the end of each session.

GOVERNOR FISHING OPENERS

In 2019 Governor Walz navigated through his first two-year budget. Near the end of session, on opening fishing in mid-May, as was the tradition, Walz invited the four legislative leaders to join him on a fishing pontoon. This traditional event served several purposes. First it showed the Minnesota public that their political leaders could get along. It also highlighted one of Minnesota's great traditions, fishing. Finally, sometimes issues got settled on the boat. This event was often just a few days before the session ended.

One time, while fishing with Governor Dayton a few years earlier, the boat guide, Kelly Morrell, asked the governor if he would help get funding for Highway 23 by Willmar, Minnesota. This was a project Republicans had been pushing for already. The governor said he would, and true to his word, he helped make sure this project was funded in the bonding bill.

Governor Dayton wasn't much at fishing. In fact he often said he repelled fish. At another Dayton fishing opener, on the Mississippi near St. Cloud, Dayton was about to be skunked again. I cast from the pontoon boat to a spot about a foot from the tip of a fallen log near shore. Wham! I had a huge strike but missed the fish. I told the guide to cast the governor's lure in the same spot, one foot from the log tip. His cast missed the mark, and there was no strike. I told the guide to do it again, one foot from the tip of the log. This time the guide hit the mark. Wham! The fish bit hard, and Governor Dayton reeled in a good-sized smallmouth bass. He gave me the credit for the fishing advice. It was fun.

In 2019, Walz's first fishing opener, we didn't solve any budget issues, but we did carry on an important tradition. Bakk, the minority leader of the Senate, and I, both fishermen from the Iron Range, mopped up in a healthy competition pitting the Senate against the executive branch and the House. Governor Walz, like Dayton before him, never claimed to be a fishing pro. He bantered back, "Let's go pheasant hunting, and I will show you what I know." It was all in good fun.

GOVERNOR WALZ INITIALLY
GOOD TO WORK WITH

The session ended shortly after that opener, almost on time. Every legislator went back home because our work was done. In the first year two years that Tim Walz was governor, people were generally satisfied with their government. The budget got done without the usual drama, both sides could claim wins, and both sides made a real effort to be civil. As a result, the governor's popularity increased, partly because of the Senate GOP's push for the successful tax reductions, but also because he cooperated where it made sense. He campaigned with a slogan, "One Minnesota," and at first it looked like he meant it.

The rest of the year, out of session with no election looming in the fall, was a time to pause and enjoy Minnesota outdoor living. It was a quiet time before an unseen storm.

Far away, in Wuhan, China, on December 12, 2019, a number of patients began to experience symptoms of a pneumonia-like illness, that eventually became known as COVID-19.

CHAPTER 13

COVID-19 AND THE MISUSE OF EMERGENCY POWERS

T HE BEGINNING OF the 2020 session, like most non-budget sessions, began uneventful, but that was about to change.

The COVID-19 pandemic will forever be etched in my mind. Everyone was touched in some way by the virus and how the world, the country, and states responded to it. It had been a long time since our country encountered a virus this significant. It was the worst in my lifetime, and many mistakes were made. Lives were at stake—not just from the virus but also how governments were going to respond to the pandemic. Some said it wasn't that serious, but it was. Fear gripped the hearts of many, and as a result, the whole world suffered beyond the damage of the virus itself.

It began, like many viruses, in a far-off land in late 2019. Wuhan, China, was reporting deaths from an unknown virus. Like many viruses in far-off lands, most Americans, including me, didn't think about it much. Even when the Centers for Disease Control and Prevention (CDC) alerted our nation in January of 2020 of the outbreak, most still had little concern.

But by March 11, 2020, with the World Health Organization (WHO) declaring a global pandemic related to COVID-19, many people were in panic mode. The next day, the first restrictions in the United States related to the virus began in New York with stay-at-home orders, or lockdowns.

PRESIDENT TRUMP TAKES EARLY DECISIVE ACTION AGAINST COVID-19

President Trump took early action to cut off travel from China because in the beginning, no one knew how bad this virus was going to be. Trump also deserves credit for launching a plan to deliver vaccines in record time as it became apparent that this was no ordinary virus. When developing a vaccine, the common practice was to do sequential testing to produce a vaccine. Trump supported efforts to do simultaneous testing instead to speed up the process—and it worked. Even so, those vaccines were not available till December of 2020, and at the time, no one thought they would even be ready that early.

What decisions would governments decide to make until vaccines were ready for those that wanted them? The desire to protect its citizens caused many in government leadership roles to take away people's freedoms to try to protect the public from the scourge of the virus, and that is when the conflicts began.

GOVERNOR WALZ STARTS OUT ON THE RIGHT PATH AGAINST COVID

On March 2, 2020, a few days after the first death in the United States from COVID-19, Governor Walz brought legislative leaders together for a private meeting to talk about what actions should be taken in Minnesota related to the virus. This was a good first move.

In the early days of the pandemic, there was significant cooperation with the legislative branch, which included a Democrat-controlled House led by Speaker Hortman and a Republican-controlled Senate led by me. We quickly passed legislation to provide over $20 million dollars to the Minnesota Department of Health for help in responding to this pandemic. Governor Walz, a Democrat, was working well with President Trump's Republican administration. Everyone was working together...until we weren't.

GOVERNOR WALZ DECLARES A STATE OF EMERGENCY

On March 13, 2020, Governor Walz declared a state of emergency in Minnesota related to the virus, granting him sweeping emergency powers. At virtually the same time, President Trump declared a national state of emergency. It became clearer that the virus was not going to be contained. Every state took some measures to combat the virus, but some took much more extreme measures than others. At first, the goal was to slow the virus down while scientists worked at warp speed to develop vaccines to combat the virus.

The governor's emergency powers allowed him to unilaterally close schools, which he started to do on March 15. He did the same thing to bars, restaurants, theaters, gyms, museums, and more on March 16 and 17.

But even then, in the beginning, there was still cooperation from both legislative bodies in Minnesota. Lawmakers in Minnesota provided another $200 million of aid to hospitals for the additional expenses they would be incurring.

Fear had set in. There was a nationwide run on toilet paper and hand sanitizer, and grocers asked customers to only buy what they needed. They had to limit the amount each person wanted to buy, assuming it was even in stock.

As schools and businesses closed, parents were now home with their kids, who were trying to learn through distance learning. It became obvious early that many students were doing very poorly with this learning method.

Businesses stepped up their efforts to help produce extra quantities of personal protective equipment, PPE. It was then announced that the 2020 Summer Olympics would be canceled. The world was shutting down.

On March 25, Governor Walz issued his first stay-at-home order that began on March 27 and was to end on April 10. It didn't end.

Even then, though disagreements began to surface, there was still bipartisan cooperation, with legislators passing another $330 million of resources in Minnesota to be available for the pandemic response. It passed with almost complete support from the legislature. At the federal level, Congress passed and President Trump signed a $2.2 trillion stimulus and relief bill to extend jobless benefits.

By April, masks were now recommended by the federal government, and everyone was practicing social distancing of six feet, with signs posted everywhere to remind everyone. The number of people recommended in elevators was also reduced.

Our state legislature was still working, but we allowed legislators to vote remotely, something that had never happened before in Minnesota. Nothing felt normal anymore.

Lockdowns Continue and GOP Pushback Begins

By April 8, 2020, Governor Walz decided to extend his stay-at-home order another three weeks. This caused a record number of people to apply for unemployment benefits. This was really when my pushback began. I knew the virus was serious, but I also knew there were many other factors that we had to measure that would be equally destructive to our society.

In addition many parts of the state had very little or no COVID-19 infections. Why have a blanket statewide lockdown? We suggested that if Governor Walz was going to demand lockdowns, to consider doing it by county or region instead of the entire state. That fell on deaf ears.

Governor Walz's COVID Decisions Hurting Minnesotans

My opposition was behind the scenes at this point. I could see that decisions meant to stop the virus had many negative consequences that had to be measured as well. Locking the public down would cripple businesses, which in turn, would literally kill some of these small businesses or drain them of any savings they had. The pressure of a failing business would affect the emotional health of those it impacted and touch the relationships around them. Locking people down would isolate many people, which in turn would be responsible for individuals developing all kinds of emotional issues. One drug addiction recovery group shared with me that many of the graduates of their program were suffering from isolation and struggling with the temptations of the addictive behavior they had overcome. Kids locked out of schools and separated from their friends were struggling emotionally, and their learning and grades plummeted.

All of these problems and more were related to the choice that too many governors across the country made to keep their states locked down. Some states took a different route, keeping their states much more open. Those states had much better results related to the non-COVID issues. The differences in COVID deaths between states like Minnesota, where Governor Walz locked everything down, and states like Wisconsin that were much more open were insignificant. But the variables outside of COVID deaths were starkly different. Wisconsin's Democratic governor also wanted to lock everything down, but the Wisconsin Supreme Court ruled that he did not have that power to do so on his own. The Republican legislature in Wisconsin did not want to lock the state down, and so it remained more open.

As data continued to come in on COVID, the divide as to the right course of action became greater, more passionate, and unfortunately, more political.

MAIL-IN BALLOTS RIPE FOR CORRUPTION

On April 8, 2020, Minnesota Secretary of State Steve Simon began pushing for an all vote-by-mail election, another policy I opposed. Blanket mail-in ballots would be ripe for corruption. Unlike absentee ballots, which require quite a bit of scrutiny, mail-in ballots sent to everyone could simply be gathered up by unscrupulous players and dropped in ballot boxes. Once the ballot was in the ballot box, it was nearly impossible to determine if it was fraudulent. We agreed to a compromise of an expansion of absentee voting but no all-mail elections. Under emergency powers, we believed the governor could have said we were going to have an all vote-by-mail election, which would have been a terrible precedent. So we compromised, agreeing to more absentee ballots and more time for the ballots to be counted.

So many problems kept jumping up as a result of Governor Walz's continued lockdown. Hospitals were forced to cancel all elective surgeries, their major profit center, to save PPE. This was a difficult issue, but I think there could have been other avenues to preserve PPE than closing down these outpatient surgery centers. What is even more hypocritical is that, by the governor's emergency declaration, these facilities were closed, but abortion clinics remained open.

By April 10, the hospital association crunched the numbers and proclaimed that they would lose $2.9 billion over the next ninety days without a change in the government-mandated close of surgery centers. They were going to need financial help.

Governor Walz was making all of these unilateral decisions based on models from the University of Minnesota. I appreciated the work they were doing, but there were multiple other models that should also have been looked at as well. I could see from other models how COVID was impacting the world. It was easy to see who was succumbing to COVID-19; the vast majority of people at risk were our elderly citizens and those who had comorbidities.

GOVERNOR PURCHASES A MORGUE THAT IS NEVER USED

Early on we tried our best to support the governor in this obvious crisis. There were decisions he made that I would express opposition to, but I did it privately. During a worldwide pandemic, I wanted to show a united front to our panicked state. One such example was the purchase of a warehouse to be repurposed as a morgue. I suggested we simply lease a building or buy freezer trucks instead. Other states were buying freezer trucks for the potential of massive deaths from COVID-19. They were far less expensive than a morgue and allowed much more flexibility. But in the end I did not prevail, and the building was never used as a morgue.

The morgue ended up never being used for body storage because the number of deaths the Walz thought was going to happen was wrong—by a lot.

DISAGREEMENT ABOUT PREDICTED DEATHS FROM COVID—WALZ WAS WRONG

During one of the early private conversations with the governor and his team, the governor said that if he locked everything down, only forty thousand to fifty thousand would die in Minnesota. Right after that, I remember messaging a frustrated individual on March 27, 2020, as I looked at the data. I responded to a constituent that I believed five thousand people would die in Minnesota from COVID.

This was my exact digital message on March 27, 2020:

> My assessment is that Covid 19 is serious but not as serious as the models they are using. In Mn the Governor thinks 40k will die even though we have sheltering in place 2 weeks at home. The cost to our livelihood will be astronomical, but by then, it's too late. My prediction for Mn is 5000 deaths, mostly over age 70. Still bad, but more like a really bad flu. We will have as many problems from foreclosures and lost jobs as we will have from the virus.[1]

I looked at multiple models to make my judgment. And one year later, the number of deaths was about five thousand people. That's still a large number, impacting mostly seniors, but it wasn't fifty thousand people. All of Tim Walz's decisions made unilaterally under emergency powers were based on models that were not accurate. Statewide lockdowns inflicted immense damage. Looking back now, there is general consensus that lockdowns didn't work, but at the time, our governor, most Democrat governors, and some Republican governors were hell-bent on lockdowns.

During those early months, the state budget also took a huge hit because of shutting everything down. I asked my communication team to help me develop questions that Bill Walsh called the Gazelka doctrine. We had to be thinking objectively about how the governor's decisions were impacting the economy. When he declared another emergency order, we could ask simple questions. Do these decisions as a state prepare us for a surge in COVID cases? Do our decisions exacerbate our budget shortfall? Do our decisions help us recover economically? At times, the answers to the questions conflicted with each other, but the unilateral decisions being made had to be objectively challenged.

FORTY-ONE STATE LEGISLATURES FRUSTRATED WITH GOVERNORS' EMERGENCY POWERS

The frustration with the governor doing too much by himself through emergency powers was not just in Minnesota. At least forty-one states, with both Republican and Democrat governors, had very little input from legislators. In fact, according to the National Conference of State Legislators (NCSL), by January of 2021 there were over three hundred state legislative bills considered nationwide that would curb a governor's use of emergency powers.

By April 2020, in growing opposition, we started building alliances to navigate the governor's lockdowns and what to do about them. My executive assistant, Matt Steele, helped me organize Zoom meetings with key pastoral figures to discuss the impact of lockdowns on churches and other places of worship.

I began to meet more often with groups that represented small business and tourism because they felt they had little input into what the governor was doing through emergency powers.

GOVERNOR WALZ MOVES THE GOALPOSTS

The governor kept moving the goalposts as to when things would reopen. On April 13 he said he would open things up when we could do five thousand COVID tests per day, but when that goal was reached, a new demand was made.

By mid-April, and for sure by the end of May, the pandemic should no longer have been considered an emergency that allowed sweeping unilateral powers, declared by one person, the governor.

The legislative branch had proven that we could pass emergency funding when needed. But if there was a true disagreement, there were no checks and balances left that would prevent a bad decision from being made by the governor.

There were so many silly rules and requirements and no one to stop them. In Minnesota, once a governor declares an emergency, if the emergency goes beyond thirty days, the only way to terminate the emergency powers without the governor's agreement is to have a majority of votes in both the House and the Senate.

HOW TO END EMERGENCY POWERS

The problem, unfortunately, is that emergency powers can become political. At that time, the Minnesota House was controlled by Democrats who politically aligned with the governor. The Senate, which I led, was controlled by Republicans. A vote by the House to end the powers would be perceived as a vote against their governor. This turned out to be a huge problem that I hope in the future will be changed. For the future emergencies, my hope is that both the House and Senate must agree for the governor's emergency powers to continue. In that way, much more accountability would be built into a governor's desire to make decisions unilaterally.

By opening fishing in May of 2020, most restrictions were still in place. Businesses were suffering, and churches were limping along. The public was frustrated, particularly outside of the Minneapolis/ St. Paul seven-county metro area. More and more of Walz's executive orders felt like edicts and were being challenged.

The governor's team finally agreed to allow the fishing opener, always in May, but encouraged people to get all their supplies locally and not stop anywhere near where they were going to fish. That decision crippled all the small businesses dependent on the fishing season in Minnesota. What's the difference if you buy your supplies next to your home or next to where you fish?

Golf was not allowed even if golfers separated by large distances. The Minnesota Zoo was closed, even the outdoor areas.

WALZ CREATES A HOTLINE TO TURN IN YOUR NEIGHBOR

Some small businesses decided to stay open out of desperation. Then Governor Walz created a hotline to turn your neighbor in, not creating a socially knit community but dividing it.

The Attorney General, Keith Ellison, started going after the small businesses violating the governor's orders to keep their businesses closed. We quipped, Why don't you go after the criminals in Minneapolis and St. Paul that are stealing cars instead of small business owners desperate to survive? Eventually I threatened the Minnesota attorney general that I would withhold his budget if he kept going after these struggling businesses.

But lists of restrictions continued to grow. For example, no in-person graduations were allowed, even outside, but drive through graduations were eventually allowed June 9.

No weddings or funerals were allowed, but the governor made an exception for a funeral for George Floyd. Why does the governor have the choice as to which funerals are important and which ones are not?

Nursing homes had to refuse guests, even as a loved one was about to die.

The Boundary Waters Canoe Area (BWCA) with federal oversight was open, but Minnesota state parks were closed by the governor's executive order.

MASK MANDATES BEGIN, BUT NOT IN THE MINNESOTA SENATE

By executive order, mask mandates were required everywhere on July 22, 2020. However, the only place the governor did not have the power to enforce a mask mandate was in the Minnesota Senate. The Senate, under my control, did not ever have a mask mandate. I encouraged people to wear a mask, but I never required them. I made the same decision with the vaccines. I encouraged people to get them, but I made sure it was a personal choice. If you take away a person's liberty for a perceived greater good, you destroy part of that person's soul. If you encourage rather than force the right behavior, you will get similar compliance without damaging the individual's autonomy.

LET'S HAVE CHURCH IN BARS

Bars were closed for months, but then, by a Walz executive decree, bars could be open for fifty people. In the same governor's decree, at the exact same time, churches could only have ten people in attendance, and whatever you do, don't sing. My wife, Maralee, had the best idea of all. She playfully said, "Let's just have church in the bars then."

Over the years, court rulings clarified that constitutionally, churches should have the same rights as other organizations have. This included the designated number of people allowed in their buildings. So if Walmart had five hundred patrons in their store, a church could have five hundred people in the church building. But the executive decision concerning church attendance did not grant them these rights and would require a court fight to challenge.

By mid-summer, national data showed the economy contracted

by almost 33 percent, and by the fall it was announced that one hundred thousand restaurants had closed during the first six months of the pandemic. Professional sports teams were planning to be open, but it was decided in most places that they could not have any fans in the stadiums.

Then, in the heart of the pandemic and lockdowns, George Floyd was killed by a police officer in Minneapolis on Monday, May 25, 2020. This was an event that shocked the entire world. The riots then shook our culture to its core.

CHAPTER 14

TIM WALZ'S RESPONSE TO THE DEATH OF GEORGE FLOYD AND THE RIOTS THAT FOLLOWED

ONDAY, MAY 25, 2020, George Floyd died at the hands of a calloused police officer.

This event, the death of George Floyd in the middle of COVID, seemed to set race relations back decades. I know that some of the underlying issues were always there, but the hate that many harbored for someone based on the color of their skin seemed to multiply greatly during that time.

George Floyd was no saint. He had been in jail numerous times from 1997 to 2005. In 2009 he pleaded guilty to aggravated robbery and went to prison to serve a five-year sentence. He was paroled in 2013. In 2019 he was arrested again, and based on the video, appeared to be in possession of pills, a similar reason with similar responses to the time he was stopped in May 2020.

George Floyd died while in police custody, outside of Cup Foods at East 38th Street and Chicago in Minneapolis, Minnesota. Derek Chauvin, the police officer in charge of the arrest, was holding down Floyd with a knee on his neck. The video showed that Floyd repeatedly stated that he couldn't breathe, before appearing to lose consciousness.

Like a wildfire blown by wind, spreading rapidly across a bone-dry forest, the video of George Floyd's death spread across the world.

As I watched the video of Floyd's death, I was angry at the police officer, Chauvin. At the same time, I was deeply grieved at the senseless death of George Floyd. The video gripped my heart. Like everyone else that watched it, I wondered why Chauvin could be so calloused. Friends of mine in law enforcement were also perplexed as to why Floyd was not rolled over after he was incapacitated, a standard safety procedure measure. Chauvin kept his knee on his neck for what seemed like a lifetime, nine minutes.

The Hennepin County Medical Examiner ruled Floyd's death a homicide, citing the cause of death as cardiopulmonary arrest. The examiner also noted that Floyd had other issues, including heart disease and fentanyl intoxication, and he tested positive for COVID-19. But he determined that those additional challenges were not the main cause of death. In the end Chauvin was convicted by a jury of his peers for the murder of George Floyd.

Floyd's death was a terrible moment in Minnesota, and so were the riots that ensued.

GOVERNOR WALZ SLOW TO REACT TO THE RIOTS

George Floyd died on a Monday. By Tuesday night the whole world knew, and rioting had begun in Minneapolis. This should have been squelched immediately, but instead it was allowed to continue by the mayor of Minneapolis and Governor Walz. They were both woefully unprepared and lacked the ability to lead.

After a tragic event of this nature, it should be expected that pro-tests would occur. It should also be expected that without proper enforcement, this situation could get out of control.

By Wednesday night rioting was rampant, and the local Target store was being looted. Angry crowds of protesters were gathering around the Minneapolis Third Precinct police station. Where were the police? Where was the Minnesota National Guard? Where was the rhetoric from the mayor and governor proclaiming that damaging your neighbor's property was unacceptable? Instead, the governor said we needed to make space for these protestors. Making space for protesters is appropriate—while not giving a single inch to rioters destroying property. Both things needed to be said, but in this case nothing serious was said about rioting.

Behind the scenes on that Wednesday, two days after Floyd's death, the Minneapolis police chief notified Mayor Jacob Frey that the situation was getting out of control. Frey called Governor Walz to request the National Guard for help. But the *governor did not act.*

As the events of that night unfolded, many buildings were set on fire. This was now a powder keg. Surely Governor Walz would get the National Guard out in full force, but he didn't.

GOVERNOR IS FROZEN

The governor is responsible for the National Guard and can also direct the Minnesota Highway Patrol into situations like these riots, but instead, he was sitting on his hands.

In addition, months before Floyd's tragic death, the Minneapolis Police Department had requested four hundred more police officers to help them do their job better. Minneapolis had eight hundred police officers at that time, but their request was turned away.

MINNEAPOLIS BURNS DOWN

By Thursday night, three days after Floyd's death, with still no action from the governor, the city was going up in flames.[1]

The Third Precinct was being assaulted, and the police were not allowed to defend it to the fullest extent of their ability. Rather than give orders to defend the police station, the mayor gave orders to evacuate the building, saying it was only "brick and mortar." Then the rioters burned the police station to the ground.[2]

Had Governor Walz reacted in a prompt manner when his help was requested, the police station would never have burned to the ground. This was a clarion call across the world to anarchists everywhere.

It was the first precinct destroyed by rioters in more than a century in America. It was more than bricks and mortar; it was a symbol of law and order. Destroying the police station emboldened anarchists everywhere. The respect for police dropped immeasurably through the whole fiasco.

On Thursday I texted the governor, telling him we needed the National Guard out in large numbers. I went on to say that what was happening was unacceptable. We can't allow anarchy. Had he acted on Wednesday, I would never have needed to pressure him, but I was upset. His responses were flippant and defensive. He told me I should call Bob Kroll, the Minneapolis police union leader. I then reached out to Bob Kroll to see if he would be open to talking to the governor. Kroll said he would. I then sent his contact information to Walz. The governor and the Minneapolis mayor had made many terrible mistakes, and it was impacting the entire world. On Thursday, three days after the death of George Floyd, the governor only had activated 190 National Guard members and 200 highway patrol officers to quell the riots. It wasn't even close to what was needed.

The governor promised then that he would intervene, but it was too late. Pandora's box was wide open.

I reached out again to Bob Kroll on Friday morning, asking him exactly what to do. He knew exactly what to do. In a text he gave me permission to share, he wrote:

> 2000 troops to start Hell 3000 if we can get them. Troops provide crowd control at various locations we can break down the numbers better if this starts rolling out. They will allow City police to resume safety and security on patrol to residence and make arrests to those responsible. Sheriffs deputies take over booking and transport procedures if these people are not taking away they will continue. Martial law until Monday

morning stay with it hard and fast and we can ease back later when consequences come into play it will deter many others.[3]

Had we done this starting a few days earlier, the rioters would have been stopped, with little damage to Minneapolis and beyond.

Who was Tim Walz listening to? Was he listening at all? Where was the governor? How could our governor be so out of touch with the police? Who better knows how to gain control of an out-of-control city burning to the ground?

TIM WALZ DOES NOT ENCOURAGE THE POLICE OFFICERS

Friday night, five days after Floyd's death, a curfew was put in place by the governor, but it was not enforced. The highway patrol and regional peace officers that came down to help staged in the basement of the Capitol. I could see the gatherings from my corner office in the Senate Office Building. I decided to go down to the basement of the Capitol and visit with all the officers staging. I was so grateful that they were there, and I hoped they would finally be allowed to take the streets back. I ran into Mike LeDoux of the highway patrol. He took me from group to group. It was important that I was there as leader of the Senate—especially because, as I later found out, in this darkest of hours for Minnesota, the governor never showed up to encourage the police.

WHERE IS THE GOVERNOR? TIME TO CALL THE WHITE HOUSE

In the Capitol basement I watched as they dressed in body armor and pads to protect themselves from potential aggressive contact with the rioters. They meant business that night. They knew it could be dangerous because more than ten thousand protesters, with rioters embedded, had taken to the streets. But the police force was never given the green light to take the streets back. Instead, on that night, a Wells Fargo bank was destroyed and more buildings were damaged. I was livid! I called my contacts at the White House and asked if Trump would intervene. Our governor was frozen; he was unwilling to act. I went on KARE 11 TV sometime after 10:30 p.m. to express my deep frustration with our governor. The news anchor, Julie Nelson, kept asking, Where is the governor? Isn't someone going to do something?

After calling the White House and doing the Kare 11 TV interview, I texted the governor just after 11 p.m. and asked him, "Where are you?"

I don't know what kind of conversations Governor Walz had with President Trump during the early rioting, but they did talk at least once during the first five days of the riots. My hope was that by lighting a fire under Governor Walz, he would take serious action to address this serious problem. You cannot allow people to destroy other people's property. Protesting is an important part of who we are as Americans, but the minute a protester starts destroying someone else's stuff, they need to be forcefully stopped.

By Saturday, a full five days after Floyd's death, the Minnesota National Guard was brought out in full force. The Minneapolis police coordinated with the highway patrol, many police officers and conservation officers from around the region, and the Minnesota National Guard to take back the streets of Minneapolis, and they succeeded. But what they implemented Saturday night was basically the plan that my Minneapolis police friend suggested days before. By then it was too late; the damage was done. The rioters destroyed over half a billion dollars' worth of private and public property. Local citizens were traumatized, and many minority-owned businesses were destroyed. The responsibility for the chaos rests squarely on the shoulders of Governor Tim Walz.

LATINO PASTOR TAKES ACTION

One Latino pastor said he organized about one hundred armed men to protect the six blocks or so that they lived in. There were no police available to help them, so they did it themselves.

At first the protesters and rioters were mostly local to the area, but as the riots progressed, rioters came from beyond Minnesota to participate. Plans were made by rioters to impact other parts of the Twin Cities and other places like Duluth and Bemidji, Minnesota.

Bemidji police officers were given intel of plans for riots in their northern Minnesota city. The Bemidji police found bricks and Molotov cocktails stashed for planned riots. One police officer, who was also a retired veteran and sharpshooter in the national guard, was put on top of the local police station to protect the building from any advancing rioters. He realized while perched on top of the building that there was no way down if the building were set on fire. He knew he would have to permanently stop someone carrying a Molotov cocktail or die himself. Thankfully he did not have to make that terrible decision.

All these events, starting with the death of George Floyd, lit a match inflaming the world, and that fire had to be put out.

As the riots began to subside, there was a chorus of angry people demanding retribution against *all* police, not the rioters. Any resolutions condemning the rioters were not supported by Democratic legislators in Minnesota. The Democrat-controlled city council of Minneapolis voted to defund the police. Democratic leaders at the legislature were demanding ridiculous police "reforms" that would hinder the men and women in blue from doing their jobs well. Rather than acknowledge that one police officer was responsible for the death of Floyd, too many people wanted all police officers to suffer.

As one of the additional tragic outcomes, a record number of police officers nationwide have been killed in the line of duty, from gunshots and assault, since the death of Floyd.

HOW TO BRING MINNEAPOLIS BACK TOGETHER

After George Floyd died, many of us were trying to make sense of it all. It was a time for soul searching and contemplative prayer. A few days after Floyd's death, I was invited to the main rioting area by Democratic Senator Patricia Torres Ray. This was way outside my comfort zone; the protesting and vandalism was still going on, although it was not as intense. I didn't want to go but felt I must go.

Matt Steele, my executive assistant, often played a key role in helping me connect to church leaders and other community leaders. He was willing to travel with me into this area of unrest and opened the door for many productive meetings.

Unlike my district, where I represented most of four rural counties, Senator Torres Ray's district was compact, a sliver of one county. I ended up trying to find her a few blocks outside of her district, but we never connected in North Minneapolis. But her invitation was the catalyst to bring me down there.

First I went to scene of the crime, now called George Floyd Square. This was before 9:00 in the morning. I had spent very little time in this part of Minneapolis, other than a funeral for a friend at Richard Coleman's church, Wayman AME in North Minneapolis. The city looked like a war zone. Boarded up and damaged buildings were everywhere. Many boarded up buildings had painted signs saying that they were minority-owned businesses, but that didn't seem to matter—they were vandalized too.

The Third Precinct police station was a charred mess. How would things ever return to normal?

GEORGE FLOYD SQUARE

I did not announce who I was, and I didn't notify the press. I just wanted to experience for myself what was happening in North Minneapolis. I had been describing the area as inner-city Minneapolis, but some said that was not considered an appropriate way to describe their location.

There was a pile of flowers circled around the spot where George Floyd died. Outside of the circle of flowers were chalk written sayings, like "Rest in peace," "Black lives matter," "George Floyd," etc.

I grabbed a piece of chalk and wrote, "LIBERTY AND JUSTICE FOR ALL," underlining ALL.

I wanted justice for all. That meant for George Floyd and his family. But it also meant justice for the police officers involved in his death. It's easy to rush to judgment, and that was not my job.

MEETING NORTH MINNEAPOLIS PASTORS

I ended up visiting that area almost a dozen times over the next few months. I visited a few times with black pastors like Bishop Richard Howell, Rev. Richard Coleman, and Rev. Jerry McAfee. We would usually meet at Rev. McAfee's church in North Minneapolis, New Salem Missionary Baptist Church, and I mostly listened as they shared stories of their struggles.

My perspective was different. My experiences were different. But we all wanted North Minneapolis to heal from this terrible moment and the ongoing challenges. It was during one of those meetings that I got the idea to draft legislation that said if you were a felon convicted of using a gun and committed another felony using a gun, you automatically got jail time. That was their idea, and it made sense to me. It did not become law, but if you are going to get illegal guns off the streets, get the criminals off the streets that are using the guns.

I took a bus ride with about eight community activists, going to various areas around North Minneapolis to survey the damage and at the same time, hear their stories.

I met Pastor Victor Martinez to talk about the challenges he was experiences in the area. I had already met Victor at the Capitol earlier. He was advocating for some sort of driver's license for illegal immigrants, or undocumented citizens, depending on your perspective.

I visited with leaders from Mad Dads, a group organized to walk the streets and encourage better behavior from the young men who were wandering around at night. It was their way of fighting the community drug problem and the social disorder their community was experiencing.

I did ride-alongs with police officers from Minneapolis and St. Paul. The police are the ones who are entrusted with keeping the peace, and I wanted to see for myself what it is like to try to police in these areas. In general I think the police are undervalued for the work we expect them to do. They are put into impossible situations where decisions must be made in nanoseconds.

THE CRY OF NORTH MINNEAPOLIS

I felt the pain of North Minneapolis. I heard their cry. This was not going to change overnight. I think the pastors I talked to had it right when they said there was a deep need for spiritual revival in their community. They were frustrated that their voices were often not the main voices of their community. In addition they were disappointed that they didn't get much help from the church community beyond North Minneapolis. That was something worth thinking about. How could more affluent churches in the suburbs build stronger long-term relationships with their brothers and sisters in North Minneapolis?

They shared some of their frustrations about the police, but they didn't hate the police; they wanted to work with them. They didn't think the police needed to be defunded, like the Minneapolis City Council was proposing, but rather improved.

Like many ongoing thorny societal issues, this one was complex. Some of the people said that the lack of fathers involved with raising their children was the main reason there was so much violence. Others said that deep generational poverty was the main culprit. Others said that there was systematic racism that kept the black community down, and the Minneapolis police could not be trusted. Others said that the schools were part of the problem because the students were not getting the good education needed to get a good job.

As I said, the challenges are complex with no easy answers.

How Can I Help?

As Rev. McAfee was sharing some of these concerns, I asked him what I could do. It's easy to say I care, but could I do anything about it? He responded, "Our young people need jobs." As I thought about that, I thought about my connection with Jason George of the 49ers. The 49ers are a blue-collar union with members that are trained to use heavy equipment. They offer many six-figure jobs, and they often do their own training.

I asked George if he would be open to meeting McAfee to see if we could create a pipeline of workers from McAfee's church, which had about two thousand members. George agreed to come to McAfee's church with me, and we had a long discussion about how to make it work.

I don't think that idea has worked yet, but we all need to keep thinking creatively about how to make more opportunities available for people that want to work. In this case part of the challenge was that the 49ers train new workers in their facility on the north side of the Twin Cities. Most of McAfee's members did not have cars and needed to use public transportation where they lived. The public transportation did not go out to the training facility. I hope they can still figure out a way to make that work.

I learned a lot over those few months. I was extended far beyond my comfort zone. It helped me in my work at the Capitol. Meanwhile, at the Capitol, many Democratic legislators were pushing for extreme policies that would hinder the work police officers do to keep our communities safe.

Governor Walz Pushes for Extreme Police Oversight

Some groups began to push for new police policies that felt like retribution toward the police. I was put into a position of just saying no to many ideas folks were proposing. I'm not against reforms to help police do their jobs better. But good police officers know what works and what does not. Too much of the legislation being passed by the Democrat-controlled House and supported by Governor Walz was counterproductive to good policing.

The pressure to go too far on police reforms didn't just come from Democratic leaders like Walz and activist groups; I also was getting pressure from prominent business corporations in Minnesota.

Everyone was feeling the heat of the moment, but changes because of heightened emotions are not a good way to legislate. One corporate lobbyist called me to recommend I make a whole bunch of reforms that I was certain would make Minneapolis less safe. Like many corporations, this company had a large employment presence in downtown Minneapolis.

I told her if I did the reforms she was requesting, there would be less of a police presence in downtown Minneapolis, and the employees of her company would no longer want to work in downtown Minneapolis. They would then ask to be transferred out of that area, and in the end, her corporation would close that location. What she was demanding would hurt Minneapolis. Her company would leave, and the only ones hurt would be the folks remaining in Minneapolis.

Another lobbyist for a group representing businesses basically delivered the same message to me. I told this lobbyist to tell his boss to go pound sand.

He was surprised by my firmness and asked, "Do you really want me to tell him to go pound sand?"

"Yes, tell him," I said.

I wasn't trying to be belligerent; I could simply see the consequences of going too far on changing how police do their work. If the police's hands are tied, if they are constantly reprimanded for trying to keep the peace in impossible situations, if they feel like no one has their backs, you can expect them to be less effective in helping us keep our communities safe.

In the end, as crime continued to rise in Minneapolis and as corporate employees felt less and less safe downtown, the business community began to change their tune. They realized that we all need good police officers.

POLICE DISRESPECTED

But actions against police continued. The Minneapolis Park and Recreation Board kicked the State Patrol out of their headquarters, where troopers used to be able to eat lunch and take breaks.[5] Then, Minnesota National Guard members were kicked out of a union hall.[6] In other actions, many metro public schools removed the school resource officers, or SROs, from their schools. Having an SRO in the school, building good relationships with the teenagers, and keeping the peace was a positive way for the police to interact with future adults.

The ranks of good police officers, particularly in Minneapolis, began to shrink. Some retired early, others went on disability for PTSD, and fewer people signed up to join the police ranks.

Where at one time the Minneapolis police department wanted to grow their numbers from eight hundred to twelve hundred, instead, the number of police in Minneapolis was down to about three hundred officers. I don't know where that number is today, but I know it's less than eight hundred. Lower numbers of police make it difficult to build relationships with the local communities. Now they must pick and choose which calls to respond to and which ones will have to wait.

Chauvin was held responsible and convicted of murder in the death of George Floyd. But why was the police profession being put on trial? Without police, you do not have continued peace. That is exactly what is happening in too many metropolitan areas around the country. As a police force fades, crime rises...every time.

As the summer of 2020 kicked in, Democrats in the House passed numerous police measures that police would have interpreted as anti-police. Senator Warren Limmer, chairman of the Senate Judiciary Committee, was a great ally in helping me stop the anti-police madness. We both agreed we would not pass any anti-police measures. If the police lobbyists, those that represent good policing, did not support a new piece of policing legislation, then we wouldn't support it either.

I looked to Brian Peters of the Minnesota Peace and Police Officers Association (MPPOA) for primary direction. But I also confirmed his positions with a few of my local police friends, like Sheriffs Michael Carr from Wadena County and Shawn Larsen from Morrison County. The policies that Democrats wanted to implement were statewide changes for problems that were primarily metro driven. I needed perspective from police who represented rural Minnesota as well as the metro area.

CAIR and Black Lives Matters Picket My Insurance Agency

Organizations like CAIR (Council on American-Islamic Relations) and Black Lives Matter pushed hard against me. They demanded I accept aggressive police "reforms." They even brought two buses full of protesters up north to picket my insurance agency in Baxter. This wasn't that many weeks after the burning of Minneapolis, so I did not take it lightly.

Senate Office Breached by Protesters

Protesters carrying Black Lives Matter signs also had forced their way into the Senate Office Building a few weeks earlier. They tricked a guard into thinking they needed help, but instead, when he cracked the door open, they forced their way in. They had just parked a car on the light rail tracks, with their sign displayed prominently. We had no idea what they were up to, but for sure, they were up to no good.

When I first got the word that they had breached the building, I had no idea how many there were or whether they were armed. Capitol security was rushing from the Capitol through the underground tunnel to the Senate Office Building to stop their advancement. It turned out they were not armed, but on my part, I was armed. I had my permit to carry, and it no longer felt like a safe place anymore. I hoped to God I wasn't put in a situation where I needed to use my gun. That event and how it made me feel reflected the time we were in.

So when CAIR and Black Lives Matter folks came to my neck of the woods, Baxter, Minnesota, I paid attention. The vast majority of citizens in my area have a great appreciation for the police. When word got out that police protesters were coming my way, a group of citizens, at least as large as the group of protesters, showed up at my office to help the police defend me and my business.

Nothing came of it, other than making a few of my clients nervous. I had been personally protested before, and I was not going to be bullied into passing legislation that I knew was not good for our state.

Back at the Senate Office Building, I could see firsthand that the Twin Cities had become less safe. One afternoon, many of us in the Senate Office Building heard a loud crash right outside our windows, between the building and the Capitol. A carjacking had occurred with an ensuing police chase and the vehicle crashing into a light pole in the governor's parking space at the Capitol. As we looked out our windows, we could see the perpetrators fleeing in multiple directions. It was hard to believe this now was the new normal in Minneapolis and St. Paul.

Another carjacking took place in the parking lot of a Lunds grocery store in Edina. The police asked me to come down and learn how the criminals were stealing cars. The perps would look for an expensive car with an elderly owner. As the owner left the grocery store and approached her car, they would block the car in with another car and aggressively take the car from its owner. This was now happening daily in Minneapolis.

The police were overwhelmed with daily crime. They didn't have a big enough force to prevent those who wanted to act out. In addition police were no longer given the benefit of the doubt when they made a mistake, but it seemed guilty until proven innocent.

DAUNTE WRIGHT KILLED

In another tragic death, Daunte Wright was shot and killed by a police officer, Kim Potter, while resisting arrest on April 11, 2021. Potter had mistakenly drawn her handgun instead of her Taser during a traffic stop. And when Wright started to flee, she pulled the trigger on her gun, instead of the Taser, and fired one shot, killing Daunte Wright.

Wright was wanted for failing to appear in court on a weapons charge. As Anthony Luckey, another officer on the scene, was attempting to arrest Wright, he got free and began to flee. That's when he was shot.

It was a terrible mistake. But did Kim Potter deserve to go to jail? I didn't think so. Chauvin was guilty in the death of George Floyd, but this was truly a terrible mistake a police officer made when trying to stop a fleeing man who had already skipped out of going to court on a weapon's charge.

If a surgeon made a terrible mistake that cost the life of one of her patients, would she go to jail? No, she would not. Instead, it would be a huge civil fine for the tragic mistake. That's what I believe should have happened here, but instead, Potter went to jail.

Just after the death of Wright, a large group of protesters showed up at the Brooklyn Center police station. Remembering what happened at the Third Precinct, that it was burned to the ground, the police were much more prepared for what could happen at the Brooklyn Center police station.

I went up to the Brooklyn Center police station during this protest. I wanted the police to know that I was not going to leave them hanging alone. This time, the Minnesota National Guard was present right away as well.

As I was talking to the commanding officer, I noticed to my right a National Guard soldier standing confidently ready. He had sunglasses on, so I couldn't see his face, but he seemed familiar. The more I looked at him, the more I thought I knew him. Suddenly it hit me—it was Senator Zach Duckworth, responding to the need to protect this precinct.

We both smiled when he realized I knew who he was. This was so typical of Senator Duckworth. He is a humble but confident warrior when needed, a statesman at the Capitol, and a good family man. I'm glad to call him my friend.

US Representative Maxine Waters Riles Up the Protesters

The day I visited the precinct is the same day Maxine Waters, a US representative from California, came to agitate the crowd. She literally said that the protesters should stay on the streets, violating the curfew. She also said the protesters should "get more confrontational"—and they did.[7] Later that night, two National Guardsmen suffered minor injuries in a drive-by shooting. The shots missed them, and they only received superficial injuries from the incident, but it could have been much worse.

Because the Third Precinct in Minneapolis was allowed to burn to the ground, this time the police were much more prepared and allowed to defend the Brooklyn Center police station. This time, when the protesters started to get violent, they were immediately surrounded by the police and arrested. Organized plans for rioting were found with some of the agitators who were arrested. I'm sure they did not think the police would act so quickly.

Why would anyone want to be a police officer anymore? Police officers getting killed, from gunshots and assault, in the line of duty is at an all-time high. Many urban communities do not respect the men and women in blue, regardless of their ethnicity. Even Minnesota's Attorney General, Keith Ellison, seemed to focus more attention on going after the police rather than the out-of-control crime in the Twin Cities. And some legislators and urban community leaders continued to put policies in place that actually are responsible for more crime because police are less effective.

This was the situation during that time. At the legislature I was willing to adopt police reforms that made sense, and as a result of genuine compromise, we did end up passing many agreed-upon police reforms. If the police could support a reform, then I could support a reform. If I had a question about a particular suggested change to procedure, I had a host of good police officers I could ask about the proposed change.

In the end we passed more reforms than had been done in a long time, but the police also supported the direction and decisions made.

But we also left many proposals in the garbage can. Some wanted to take away qualified immunity from an individual police officer. Basically the local community that hires a police officer is responsible for paying the cost of any negligence resulting from their police work. If an individual police officer is responsible for carrying his own professional liability, it would be cost prohibitive to being a police officer. It is not a high-paying job like being a surgeon, for example. Where a surgeon does have to generally pay for professional liability for any mistakes made, the surgeon can afford it; the police officer can't.

Another "reform" was the idea of putting a citizen board *above* the police board to tell police how to police. We don't do that in any other profession. Attorneys have a board run by attorneys. The medical board is full of doctors. The people that best know how to police are people that must do it.

My hope is that we learn from the death of George Floyd and the riots that came after. I for one wanted to learn more than what I knew. As I mentioned, I went down to the site where Floyd died and met community leaders. I also prayed with folks who were onsite, asking God to intervene.

The time I spent in North Minneapolis helped me develop some good relationships with black and Latino pastors from Minneapolis. I walked with Mad Dads and listened to their stories. I visited countless people on both sides of this thorny issue. I have done ride-alongs with Minneapolis and St. Paul police officers. Maralee and I even attended the funeral for George Floyd. I'm listening, and I will continue to learn more.

Since COVID, the death of George Floyd, and the riots that followed, our nation seems to be struggling to find its way.

Where Was God in All This?

In my role as leader—now more so as the governor's opposition rather than partner—I was struggling to find answers. Where was God in all this? The crisis was monumental: the COVID pandemic first and then the riots in North Minneapolis.

The Senate GOP caucus began a lot more meetings with prayer during this time. We were in a crisis, and the answers were difficult to find.

During this time, my wife's prayerful intercession took the form of painting. While praying, she drew a sketch of an innocent little girl. The sketch portrayed the crisis through the eyes of a little girl, innocence lost; it was haunting. Her desire was for adults to see what was happening from the perspective of a child.

Senate Hearings Confirm National Guard Could Have Prevented Riots

In the end Governor Walz responded terribly during this crisis. The Senate held hearings later that summer on July 9, 2020, to review the details of what happened. Senator Scott Newman was point on the hearings. Many testified, but the most compelling testimony came from General Jon Jensen, leader of the Minnesota National Guard. He was asked if earlier mobilization of the National Guard by Governor Walz would have prevented rioting and damage. His answer: "My unprofessional opinion as it relates to law enforcement is yes. My professional military opinion is yes."[8]

Had Governor Walz called up the Guard on Wednesday, when Mayor Frey of Minneapolis asked the governor for help, it is highly probable that much of the damage would have been prevented. The governor still blamed Mayor Frey months later, but the responsibility resides with Tim Walz, and he failed.

WALZ FLIPPANTLY CALLS GUARD MEMBERS "19-YEAR-OLD-COOKS"

Even when confronted with the truth that he delayed his response and that he should have acted more decisively two days after the death of George Floyd, he simply quipped, "I don't think the mayor knew what he was asking for." Walz said, "I think the mayor said, 'I request the National Guard, this is great. We're going to have massively-trained troops.' No, you're going to have 19-year-olds who are cooks!"[9]

To the broader issue of race relations, the tragic death of George Floyd, and what to do now, I can simply say that I want to be part of the solution. These issues are complex and don't fit into neat sound bites. I pray that Martin Luther King Jr.'s dream, that people "will one day live in a nation where they will not be judged by the color of their skin but by the content of their character," will be our nation's reality.[10] Until then, we all need to keep striving toward those ideals.

CHAPTER 15

GOVERNOR WALZ LETS STATUE OF CHRISTOPHER COLUMBUS BE TORN DOWN BY A MOB

I N THE MIDST of COVID and the George Floyd riots, Governor Walz again frustrated me by allowing the statue of Christopher Columbus on the Minnesota Capitol grounds to be torn down by a small group of protesters.

I was having a meal in downtown St. Paul outside a restaurant at a sidewalk table on June 10, 2020. My quiet meal was interrupted by an urgent call from a friend at the Senate Office Building. He told me that a small group of protesters was trying to pull down the statue of Christopher Columbus. I was just a mile or so away, so I asked for the check and bolted out to my car to get back to the Capitol. As I arrived at my Senate office suite on the southeast corner of the third floor, a flatbed truck was leaving the area with the statue of Christopher Columbus sprawled on the back of the flatbed. How could this happen? Why was the flatbed truck on the scene so quickly? Was this coordinated? I was angry, and the more I heard about what happened, the angrier I got. We are a country of laws, not mobs. But lately, too many people, frustrated by various positions on either side of the political aisle, are taking matters into their own hands. We cannot allow this to be the new normal.

Nationally, especially after the recent death of George Floyd, it had become a craze to illegally remove historical statues around the country. Mobs or individuals were destroying or defacing statues of Columbus, Washington, Jefferson, Abraham Lincoln, and others. The premise for destroying these monuments was that these historical figures were guilty of unspeakable atrocities, that they grabbed land that belonged to others, and now they must be held responsible for their actions.

SOME OF AMERICA'S PAST IS DISGUSTING

It is true that parts of the America's history are disgusting and hard to believe. There are many flaws of the European settlers that I can point to—condoning slavery, murdering innocent indigenous people and breaking treaties with them, mistreating many immigrant communities that came here for a better life, etc.

But I could point to the same flaws for domination from virtually any people group in any era of civilization. Before European settlement came to the United States, indigenous tribes were at times at war with each other to determine dominance. The Sioux were in much of Minnesota but were driven west by the Ojibwe people.

Part of my own national heritage comes from an area that was once called Prussia, a land encompassed today by Germany and Poland. The Prussians were a people group that was completely eliminated after World War I. Mankind has always been at war with each other somewhere in the world.

Another atrocity in America was slavery. Slavery, at the time, was a worldwide phenomenon that had been around for thousands of years. It was never right, but it was commonplace in the first few centuries of America. We should never forget this terrible sin upon our land, but also thank God that we were one of the early nations to eliminate a millennia-long atrocity.

WE ARE ALL FLAWED PEOPLE

As to individual sins, the only sinless person was Jesus Christ, no one else. Even all my heroes were flawed. George Washington and Thomas Jefferson had slaves, and Martin Luther King Jr. was rumored to be a serial adulterer, as was Ronald Reagan in his early adult life. Really, I only have to look at my own life to see plenty of flaws.

What's my point? All of mankind is beautiful but also flawed. Any people group can produce amazing beauty and, at the same time, be guilty of unspeakable crimes against their fellow man.

I don't deny the flaws. We must learn from mankind's mistakes, but I also choose to focus on our achievements and positive character traits while learning from our mistakes.

There are some atrocities, like the slaughter of six million Jews in Europe during World War II, that must be marked with some sort of monument. We should never forget those things while we seek the best version of ourselves as a nation or individually.

But statues in America typically focus on positive achievements or character traits of an individual or group. Monuments were meant to mark a lesson learned, an important event, or an individual's positive characteristics, all for future generations to remember. We must resist those that want to illegally remove our monuments. If after careful discussion, through the legal process, the decision is made to remove a monument, then I accept that process. But illegal mob actions must be aggressively resisted.

That brings me to June 10, 2020, and the fall of Columbus at the Minnesota Capitol.

MIKE FORCIA DECLARES COLUMBUS STATUE WILL BE PULLED DOWN

It was only a small group of protesters, organized by Mike Forcia, a longtime activist. He was an early activist with the American Indian Movement, a group dedicated to advocating for indigenous people's rights. At times, the protests he was involved with were peaceful, but at other times, they were not.

On the morning of June 10, Forcia announced on Facebook his intention to tear the statue of Columbus down. He also invited the Hmong and Somalia immigrant communities to join him. The governor was made aware of this very real and open threat.

GOVERNOR WALZ FAILED TO ACT BUT KNEW THEY WERE COMING

Let me be clear: the governor knew they were coming. So did the commissioner of public safety, a former cop.[1] They had plenty of time to prepare. As the small group of protesters marched up the road toward the statue, *one* highway patrol officer was posted alongside the statue.

The Minnesota Capitol itself houses scores of highway patrol officers, but only one was outside next to the statue. The officer was having a conversation with Forcia, who was holding a rope, ready to tear down the statue if allowed. For reasons I cannot easily explain, the police officer left his post. No one was assigned to protect the statue. Immediately after the police officer left his post, Forcia had the rope about the Columbus statue, and it was pulled off its platform and came crashing to the ground. Great cheers arose from the group of protesters as Forcia, in triumph, put his foot on the neck of the Columbus statue.[2]

Within minutes that statue was on a flatbed truck, hauled to an unknown Department of Transportation building, where it lay on the floor for some time thereafter.

There were no immediate arrests. The governor said he did not condone the act, but by his lack of leadership and looking the other way, he allowed it to happen. The lieutenant governor, of indigenous decent, said she was not sad the statue was gone. She cited some of Columbus's alleged atrocities as her justification.[3]

CHRISTOPHER COLUMBUS ACCUSED BUT EXONERATED BY THE KING

There is not a lot of documentation from the 1400s, but Columbus was accused by rivals of sexually trafficking young indigenous girls. In fact Columbus made his case to the king and queen of Spain at that time and the charges were dropped.[4] In addition he spoke against this behavior and said that a great number of men who traveled to the Indies were not worthy of baptism, meaning he did not condone their actions, but rather chastised them.

In my own political career, rivals have created false stories about me that continue to live on in social media. As much as one tries to present the truth, those interested in nefarious outcomes don't really care about the truth. Regardless of what is true and what is not, Columbus was the beginning of the European settlement of America, and that should be acknowledged.

As I mentioned, Forcia was not initially charged. But after a while, he was. I believe it was because of the indignation of many as to how it happened. Forcia was charged and agreed to one hundred hours of community service as his penalty. But the statue was never put back on its pedestal on the Capitol grounds.

GOVERNOR AT FAULT

I believe the primary fault is not the folks that tore the statue down but the governor's unwillingness to stop a lawless act. You cannot allow lawlessness to be the way you govern. You cannot let people destroy more than a half a billion dollars' worth of private and public property in Minneapolis after the terrible death of George Floyd. But if they do, you must impose serious penalties for doing so.

The irony of Forcia's protest act and inviting new immigrant communities to join him is that the statue was given to the state in 1931 from an earlier immigrant group, the Italians. In the early 1900s, millions of Italian immigrants came to the shores of the United States, and many ended up in Minnesota. Italians from northeast Minnesota conceived the idea to gift a statue of Christopher

Columbus to the state as a way of combating the intense discrimination the Italian people were experiencing in the United States during that era.[5]

In October of 1931 the majestic, ten-foot bronze statue was placed on the grounds of the Minnesota Capitol. As many as thirty thousand people, many of whom were Italian, attended the unveiling ceremony. A large black-and-white photo of this event is prominently displayed at Mancini's restaurant in downtown St. Paul. Mancini's relatives were in attendance and can be seen in the photo. The original inscription declared, "To Christopher Columbus, Discoverer of America."

Later that year, in 1931, Columbus Day became a state holiday. It was a momentous occasion for many but especially for the Italian community of Minnesota.

In 1992, five hundred years after Christopher Columbus discovered this amazing land for the Europeans, a second plaque was added, crediting Coumbus with "the merging of the cultures of the old and new worlds; thereby changing forever the course and history of mankind."[6] I appreciate this additional inscription. It acknowledges that Columbus was an important figure in the beginning of what we now lovingly call America, but it also acknowledges that indigenous people groups were already here and bring value to the nation we have become.

TODD FINNEY

I had a conversation with my friend, Todd Finney from the Oglala Lakota and Wahpekute Dakota people, about Columbus Day. He asked if I was open to an indigenous day. I said, "If it does not replace Columbus Day, I would support it." In other words, I don't want Columbus Day removed. It represents the beginning seeds of the nation we would become. But I also believe that we should acknowledge the contributions of our indigenous brothers and sisters. Why does it have to be one or the other?

Todd has become a good friend. We met and prayed at the quadriga, or four golden horses, near the top of the Capitol. Afterward he said that visit to the Capitol was the first positive experience he had related to our Capitol. Years earlier government officials returned to his family a scalp from one of his ancestral fathers. I can't imagine how some of that generational trauma might impact him today. What I can do is acknowledge it happened and seek to understand.

As I have mentioned already, Columbus was an imperfect man. But so were George Washington, Thomas Jefferson, and Martin Luther King Jr, and so am I. In fact, everyone I know has one flaw or another. We don't celebrate imperfections; we honor and celebrate high achievements from imperfect people. We should all aspire to be the best version of ourselves.

Governor Walz should put the statue of Christopher Columbus back on its pedestal at the Minnesota Capitol. It was donated by the Italian community long ago, and thousands came out to celebrate its significance.

I don't think it's ever appropriate for a mob to remove or deface a monument because they disagree. In the end, in a constitutional republic, only by the rule of law should changes of that kind of significance be made—not by a mob and not by the executive branch looking the other way. These kinds of changes should only be made by the voice of the people, and that is the legislative branch.

America is and always was meant to be a pluralistic society. We need to focus on how to be more inclusive, not exclusive. That does not mean that we all agree on everything. Nor does it mean we penalize folks who do not agree with us. It means we make room for as many differences as possible.

There will be some differences that we will constructively fight for that seem irreconcilable. Some issues define the soul of our country. Those are much tougher to solve. But if our founders, on September 17, 1787, could establish a more perfect union, with some of the states embracing slavery and some of the states opposed to slavery, we can find a way to solve our differences as well. Eventually, allowing slavery in the beginning led to a civil war to end this terrible scourge. But even slavery did not stop us from forming this amazing country.

THANK GOD FOR AMERICA

I thank God for this great country and our unsurpassed success. I will not deny our terrible flaws but rather, learn from them. We have been blessed and bless many nations. We have enjoyed amazing prosperity in comparison to the rest of the world. We have given unprecedented freedoms to the individual. We have unleashed amazing creativity that has made people's lives around the world much better because of our inventions. Inventions like the telephone, electric lights, airplanes, sewing machines, cotton gins, and many more all came from American ingenuity. My hope is that we will continue in the God-given prosperity, and when we make future mistakes, like the mistakes of old, we learn from them.

CHAPTER 16

GOVERNOR WALZ AND COVID MASK MANDATES

As COVID-19 CONTINUED throughout the summer of 2020, there was a gradual opening of small businesses, but rumors were percolating that public schools would still not be open in the fall. Data clearly showed that children were less at risk from COVID-19 than the common flu. Yet, unlike a flu epidemic, where local school districts decided the best course of action, the governor made school closure decisions for the entire state. Even worse, kids were still required to wear masks in school.

BOY BURSTS INTO TEARS

I remember talking to a parent who shared the struggles his son was having in school. First, he was unnecessarily kept out of school for over a year in Minnesota, and then when the governor started allowing children back into the classrooms, children were required to wear a mask in school. This boy's dad recognized how distraught his son was, day after day, coming home from school. He asked his son what was going on. He probed with questions, trying to figure out why his son was struggling. He finally asked, "Is it the mask that you have to wear?"

His son burst into tears, and when he could finally speak, he said, "I can't see what people are feeling; all I see is blank faces." I doubt this was the only child that struggled with his everyday connections because of the mask. It was so bad that even high school athletes were required to wear masks during the sport they were playing. It's hard to believe that people could not see the danger of not getting enough oxygen while competing with a mask on.

The data clearly showed that the virus was most dangerous for the elderly and not children. In fact, for a year or so, less than a handful of students died from the COVID virus in Minnesota. As I said earlier, more school age kids died from the flu then from the COVID virus, and yet the governor shut all the schools down and didn't reopen them for what seemed like an eternity.

Governor Responded in Fear, Not Courage

The argument was, we can't be wrong—but that was fear speaking. This was a time for courage. This was a time to look at all the facts and all the consequences and make tough decisions about a very real and dangerous virus.

We had to be able to consider the mental health consequences of keeping kids out of school for multiple years. We had to consider the consequences of small businesses going bankrupt and families losing their life savings as a result. We had to think about those that struggle with addiction and how isolation would impact them. We should have considered how important it was for people to attend places of worship and community gatherings, like weddings and funerals. Fear drove some governors to shut everything down and only think of the consequences of the physical attacks of the COVID-19 virus.

My role as leader of the Senate was at first to support the governor through this chaotic time. We needed to unite, but as the governor continued to go further and further in a direction that I thought harmful to our state, my role became more combative. I was always respectful, but I needed to be diplomatically firm and proclaim that the course he was on was going to cause more damage than good.

September 2020 COVID-19 Deaths

By the end of September it was announced that 2,004 people had died from COVID in Minnesota, but that number was nowhere near Walz's early projections. In addition, at the same time, the number of deaths in Wisconsin, which was much more open, had very similar deaths to Minnesota.[1]

Incognito in Wisconsin

Simply looking at the data between Wisconsin and Minnesota would have been enough to know that Minnesota's governor went too far—but that data didn't matter. When restaurants were closed in Minnesota, a few legislators and staff, including me, for sanity's sake, would go over to Hudson, Wisconsin, to get a burger and socialize with happy people. It inevitably put us in a better mood. I tried to go incognito, and my team laughed at my approach, thinking no one would notice me in a Wisconsin bar. As they continued to laugh, my face splashed up on the TV screens for everyone to see. We all laughed then. I wasn't trying to be cavalier. I wanted our governor to be successful during the pandemic. I believe Minnesota's governor and all other governors were trying to do the best they could. But I could see the bad consequences of unilateral decisions, and it was my responsibility as leader to respectfully resist and confront.

Fear, particularly in the metro areas, was palatable for many, but it was not based on reasoning out all the ramifications to one's existence. I remember being in a boat on Gull Lake in central Minnesota in the summer of 2020 and trolling by another boat whose driver, in the middle of the lake, had a mask on. In another example, I saw a picture of a motorcyclist wearing a mask but not wearing a helmet. I can tell you as a motorcyclist, the risk of a head injury is a lot greater than catching COVID outdoors. The mask, for some, was a psychological way of feeling protected from a virus they couldn't see but constantly heard about. Each day, the new death numbers were posted with more of the latest bad news. This constant stream of bad news was not good for our national psyche.

COVID-19 Was Real and Dangerous

On the other hand, some thought the COVID-19 virus was not really that dangerous. I was not in that camp. I talked to many health-care professionals on the front line who were treating the worst cases of COVID-19. It was clear that in some places, our healthcare providers were overwhelmed and getting worn out. To the average person, not infected and not connected to someone who had one of the dangerous cases of COVID, it could have been perceived as a complete overreaction. That's why, even now, I can affirm the virus was clearly potentially dangerous. It was difficult to manage care for the group of infected patients that were in life-threatening situations. But if you were not near the hospitals, you really didn't comprehend the scope of the impact.

The basics of avoiding the COVID-19 virus should have been encouraged, like we would for any other type of virus. You should cover your cough, wash your hands, avoid indoor congested areas, stay home if you are sick, and if you want to, wear a mask or isolate yourself if you are in an at-risk category. But forcing people to wear a mask, shelter in place, or even get an eventual vaccine was going too far.

At first Governor Walz, like most Democratic governors, chose severe measures to slow down the virus while we waited for vaccines to be developed. But somehow that morphed into the thought that he could somehow stop the virus. The lockdowns kept being extended. But those extreme measures tightly wound society, creating a very scared and frustrated population.

TIME FOR EMERGENCY POWERS TO END

As I mentioned already, by mid-May 2020, many of us no longer felt like this was an emergency requiring Tim Walz to have dictatorial emergency powers. Instead, it was a pandemic that the executive branch and the legislative branch needed to face together. Working together included checks and balances that prevented unilateral decisions that one side considered too far.

At this time, the Senate in Minnesota voted to end emergency powers for the governor, but the House, controlled by Democrats, would not agree. We were stuck. The governor wanted to keep the powers, and House Democrats aligned with the governor.

Under my leadership, Senate Republicans began to push back publicly. Almost every month going forward, we voted to end emergency powers. The House disagreed.

I asked Senator Scott Jensen and others to be more active at confronting the constant drumbeat from the governor, proclaiming that science says we need to do this or that related to COVID. Scott is a medical doctor and could counter the narrative the governor continued to create.

TIME TO REMOVE COMMISSIONERS

One of the few levers we had left was the Senate's power to remove commissioners that the governor appointed but were yet unconfirmed. I had already warned the governor about a few commissioners that were not doing their job well. This was not a path I wanted to take, because I knew it would drive the governor and I further apart.

The power to remove a commissioner should not be taken lightly. Only fifteen or so commissioners had been removed through the Senate process in Minnesota since the 1930s. The warnings I gave the governor earlier about their performance was my attempt to get them to improve and be accountable the legislative branch, not just to the executive branch.

Now uncontrolled emergency powers were put into the mix,

and we needed to explore this lever to get the governor's attention. If there are not thirty-four of the sixty-seven senators in the Minnesota Senate that are willing to confirm a commissioner, that commissioner is removed if brought to a vote on the Senate floor.

Some Republican senators were demanding that I remove a commissioner a week until the governor relinquished his emergency powers. That was too extreme and would destroy the primary reason senators have the power to confirm or remove a commissioner—because they are not doing their job. If we went that route, and the roles were reversed sometime in the future, then a Democratic Senate majority would remove a Republican governor's appointments for frivolous reasons.

Because I thought about future ramifications, I proceeded, but cautiously. First we removed Nancy Leppink of the Department of Labor and Industry, with thirty-four Republican senators agreeing. A little while later we removed Steve Kelley from the Department of Commerce. In his case we did not have thirty-four GOP votes to remove him. The only way it was going to happen was if I found Democratic legislators to also support the removal. Kelley had been difficult on several northeast Minnesota projects and at odds with the Democratic legislators in that area. Over time, I was able to convince those legislators that it was worth removing him. Once we brought the vote to the floor, which I would not have done unless I had the removal votes, the Republican senator that was in opposition also now supported removal. Most legislators don't want to be the only one voting against the will of their caucus. It draws unnecessary attention to them, and depending on the issue, it may invite a challenge to their position as legislator from someone in their own party.

Both of those commissioners were removed because they were not doing their job well, but our hopes were that it would also start a serious conversation about the end of emergency powers. It didn't. But it did cause the governor to be much less cavalier about the decisions he was making, because he knew we could take out more commissioners if we wanted to. The commissioner of the

Department of Natural Resources resigned rather than face the possibility of being removed for pushing an agenda we specifically asked her not to.

Three times I forced out a governor-appointed commissioner. All of these took place when the governor was running the state under emergency powers. I always had a conversation with the governor ahead of time, in fact multiple times each, before I put the hammer down.

I didn't enjoy removing commissioners, but sometimes it had to be done. I remember being on conservative talk radio after we forced out one of them. The host was gleeful for the removal, and I agreed it needed to be done, but I was not gleeful. I was impacting a real person's life. The commissioner had a family and was not just some chess piece on a chessboard. I've never enjoyed firing someone, but sometimes it must be done.

You have to know yourself as a leader. Sometimes you build a bridge, sometimes you need to build a wall, and sometimes you throw a bomb. I was best at building bridges. But sometimes a bridge builder needs to be a bomb thrower, and vice versa. I was comfortable being the majority leader, but I don't think I would have been a great minority leader. In that position, part of your task is to regularly and publicly point out the weaknesses of the bills the majority is trying to pass. On the other hand, the Senate majority leader gets to paint the vision of the direction he plans to chart. But because I was not a great bomb thrower, I made sure I had some people around me who were better at it than I was. That created the right tension for me not to be too soft on my adversary.

PRESIDENT REAGAN FORGED FRIENDSHIPS WITH ADVERSARIES

Some say that we should never reach out to our adversaries with genuine warmth, but President Ronald Reagan showed us that building true friendships with adversaries can be a meaningful connection with positive results. That does not mean that making friends is the ultimate goal. But if it appears that our adversary is a person of good character, it might naturally occur if we are willing to take a risk.

President Ronald Reagan was tough, but he built bridges. As president, his political adversary was Speaker of the House Tip O'Neill. They were political opposites but somehow managed to form a genuine friendship based on mutual respect and a common love for America. Together they made it work and passed meaningful legislation.[2] They genuinely liked each other, which turned out to be a good thing for our country.

REAGAN BUILDS FRIENDSHIP WITH MIKHAIL GORBACHEV OF THE SOVIET UNION

Another unique friendship Reagan had was with Mikhail Gorbachev of America's archenemy, the Soviet Union. He told Soviet Union President Mikhail Gorbachev he was part of an evil empire and that he needed to tear down the Berlin Wall, dividing West Germany from East Germany—and he eventually did it. Together, they made the world a safer place, and that end result was because they too had a genuine friendship.[3] Later Gorbachev spent time with President Reagan at Reagan's ranch in the foothills above Santa Barbara, California.

Speaking of Reagan's ranch, I had the opportunity to visit it a couple of times. The ranch has been preserved as it was when Reagan was president. Visiting the ranch really helped me appreciate the secret to Ronald Reagan's success: his humility. He was confident and articulate, but humility was unique to his greatness. Ronald Reagan spent over 365 days of his two terms as president at this ranch, dubbed the Western White House. The ranch house was very simple. The counters were made of Formica. The king-size bed for the Reagans was two twin beds zip-tied together. Reagan put a footrest on the side where he slept so his feet would not hang out too far over the end. But the ranch was where Ronald Reagan could return to a normal life, cutting wood, riding horses, and making fences. It was part of his secret to a successful presidency.

More than once, the folks maintaining the ranch told Reagan that they would be happy to complete the projects not yet done on the ranch. Reagan pushed back, saying the projects were part of the reason he came back to the ranch. They allowed him to take his mind off the weight of being president, even if only for a few moments.

The Soviets usually knew when he was there too. I was told by a ranch historian that later Reagan found out they had a nuclear sub parked off the coast, with the ability to quickly strike the ranch if needed. I'm glad the world took a different route.

WALZ BLUNDERS

Like Reagan and Tip O'Neill, I had that kind of relationship with Democratic Governor Dayton, and my relationship with Governor Walz started that way. But with COVID emergency powers, he became a different person. He didn't listen much, including to some Democratic legislators I know. He acted more like a king and as a result, unnecessarily blundered too many times.

I pushed hard against the governor and his actions during COVID and the riots after the death of George Floyd. But even then I tried diplomacy first. But when he didn't listen, my rhetoric was more negative, and people listened.

CHAPTER 17

POLITICAL FIGHT CONTINUES WITH GOVERNOR WALZ

C OVID-19 AND EMERGENCY powers changed the way I interacted with Governor Walz. Where once we were generally working toward common solutions we both could live with, the lengthy use of emergency powers drove us apart. I forced out three of his commissioners. We didn't talk nearly as much. I now regularly did press conferences pointing out mistakes he was making and not taking responsibility for.

SHOULD WE REMOVE COMMISSIONER MALCOLM?

Probably the most high-profile commissioner that was not removed was Health Commissioner Jan Malcolm. She was the governor's chief advisor on COVID-19 and recommended what kind of action should be taken related to stopping the virus.

The chorus of public frustration against her continued to rise to a fevered pitch from those most against lockdowns and mask mandates. GOP senators were never all in agreement that she should be removed. Some, for various reasons, were opposed to her removal at one time and supportive of her removal later. In many GOP Senate caucus meetings, one or more legislators begged us to remove her. But in the end, even if I wanted to, we could not remove her.

So as the public furor from the right rose to remove Malcolm, I never responded by bringing her confirmation to the Senate floor for a vote. Had we done that, without having the votes to remove her, she would have been confirmed, not removed. It was better to leave her unconfirmed with the possibility of removal in the future.

Some activists demanded to know which Republican senators would not remove Malcolm, and I would not tell them. Our caucus discussions were confidential.

Like other caucus decisions, I took responsibility for those decisions and the heat that followed when folks disagreed. That's what a legislative leader should do. If the leader is not the voice of his caucus, sooner or later, he won't be the leader. It is often a dance, getting your team to the right place, and it was usually a lot slower process than I would have preferred. But we had a solid team, and I was honored to lead our narrow Republican majority in the Minnesota Senate.

SHOULD WE WITHHOLD THE BONDING BILL?

There were only a few levers we could use under emergency powers. Besides removing commissioners, we could decide not to pass a bonding bill. I certainly was pressured to do that by my political base and some generous donors, but the only people that would be harmed by not doing a bonding bill were the communities asking for help from the state for their regional projects. Armchair quarterbacks told their followers to contact me about not doing a bonding bill, but I knew it would not have moved the governor to end his sweeping emergency powers. They swamped my personal cell phone with texts and calls telling me what to do.

During the session, many facts got texted to my personal phone to help me make decisions as leader. When the "conservative" activists chose that route, swamping my personal phone with texts and calls, it made it hard to get all the information from my own team in the middle of negotiations. I started calling a few of the misinformed angry folks that left messages on my phone. When I explained the situation, they appreciated that I took the time to call them. However, this was not good use of my time. I just wanted to know if their minds could be changed with factual information. Some of them did change their minds when they got the facts.

Working with the House

It was helpful to have a cordial working relationship with the Democratic House, led by Speaker Hortman. We both felt like money should be spent through the legislative branch. So when the governor was given $300 million to spend on his own through the federal CARES Act, we pushed back together. In the end our governor agreed to only spend $50 million of $300 million on COVID-related expenses with no oversite from the legislative branch. This agreement, to let the legislative branch in Minnesota spend most of the CARES Act money, was a positive attempt to work together, and apparently that was not the norm among spats with other governors.

The governor in Minnesota agreed to release $250 million of the CARES Act money back to the legislative process, and he kept $50 million for emergency COVID needs. For perspective, the Republican-controlled Wisconsin legislature got none of the CARES Act money back from their Democratic governor; he spent it all.

Churches Resist Governor Walz's Edict

The pushback on executive orders ratcheted up. When the governor said bars could have fifty people and churches could have ten, it was time to act on that front. Because I had the privilege of convening

Zoom meetings with one hundred or so faith leaders about proper courses of action, I knew they would not accept this edict.

Virtually all these leaders wanted to work with the governor, but eventually came to place that they decided they were going to open their churches without his permission. Some of them sent a cordial letter to the governor telling him of their intentions. That probably came as a surprise to the governor, but it did bring him back to the table. In the end, they agreed to compromise with a maximum of 250 people at a service.

The COVID issue split many churches right down the middle. Some parishioners wanted to stay home, some wanted to come to church and not wear masks, and some wanted to come to church and have everyone wear a mask. Each church had to grapple with the right decision for their congregations, but in the end, it needed to be their decision, not the governor's.

PRESIDENTIAL ELECTION

Added to the challenges of COVID and the death of George Floyd, we also had a hotly contested election to determine the president of the United States and control of Minnesota's House and Senate.

Trump campaigned in Minnesota throughout the fall of 2020. We ended up meeting President Trump a few times as he exited Air Force One. We also met Vice President Pence when he visited Minnesota, flying in on Air Force Two. Everyone time we were scheduled to meet them, we had to quickly find a local hospital that could give us a COVID test to make sure we were not infected with COVID-19 when we visited them.

COVID produced many aggressive responses from governments around the world. In the United States, Trump supported a trillion dollars of stimulus money to infuse into our economy. As a result, by October, the US Commerce Department said the economy had bounced back and grew 33 percent in the third quarter. That should have been the end of the stimulus packages. But under President Biden the following year, more stimulus packages were passed that juiced the economy too much and helped cause the worst inflation in decades. Combine the "free" money with supply-chain problems because of lockdowns, and our government created a huge recipe for wealth loss across the country.

Then came the November election. Minnesota, like the rest of the country, had huge outdoor gatherings to see President Trump. The riots after the death of George Floyd had huge gatherings as well. Surprisingly to some, the outdoor gatherings, without masks, didn't seem to impact the COVID infections much.

TRUMP LOST THE ELECTION IN MINNESOTA, BUT MINNESOTA SENATE GOP WON

Trump lost the election in Minnesota, and yet the Minnesota Senate squeaked by with another victory. We had now won the majority three out of the last four elections, when Senate Republicans had not won the majority before that in over forty years.

One of the reasons why I believe we won again when Trump lost in Minnesota by a large margin was that we continued to go door to door for support for our legislative candidates. The Senate Democrats decided not to go door knocking. We knew it was not a risk, but they felt it was—and it cost them. As we approached a constituent's door and knocked, we would step back a bit more. When the constituent came to the door, we asked if it was all right if we talked about the Senate candidate. If they said yes, we would give them more information. If they said no, we thanked them and moved on.

As the election results came out on election night, November 3, 2020, I was grateful that the Senate GOP retained the majority in a Democrat wave election. We added two new freshmen senators that night, Julia Coleman and Zach Duckworth. Both were suburban candidates, and both showed real promise as future leaders of the Senate GOP. I wondered how they would perceive serving as senators; it was so different during the COVID pandemic than what was normal in prior years.

COVID Senate Floor Procedures

During the COVID pandemic, when the Senate was convened, we limited the number of senators that could be on the Senate floor at one time. We used various rooms around the Senate floor for senators to gather in during the live session. We added TVs in each room so that even if you were not on the Senate floor, you were aware of what was happening. I gave up part of my majority leader suites for some of the senators to meet in. When it was time to vote, President Miller would open the voting board, and senators on the floor would vote. At the same time, Miller would ask each group of senators in various rooms to come and vote, never exceeding the maximum number of senators allowed on the floor. Then he would ask for the votes of those who were voting remotely. Each side had a designated remote vote counter. Senator John Jasinski was often the one who contacted each remote GOP voter to get their vote, either aye or nay.

It was a cumbersome process, but that was how we did it during the COVID-19 pandemic. Some Democrat senators did not want us to meet as much as we did, but I felt that if we thought businesses like Walmart were essential to be open, certainly the legislative bodies should be open as well.

Senator Jerry Relph Dies from COVID-19

The most painful memory for me related to COVID-19 was the death of my good friend Senator Jerry Relph. Senate Republicans squeaked out another one-vote majority in the fall of 2020. We had lots to be grateful for and celebrate. Trump, and pretty much everyone else in Minnesota that was affiliated with Republicans lost, but we won anyway. As is usual, leadership was selected within a few days after the election. We decided to hold our Senate

Republican leadership elections and a celebration dinner a couple of days after the general election.

COVID SUPER-SPREADER

We squeezed more than one hundred folks into a dining facility in St. Paul. At the time, gatherings of 250 were allowed. The general protocol was that you were required to wear a mask until you were eating or drinking. Less than two days earlier, many of us were gathered with our own groups of supporters, monitoring the elections. At least one person that had been at gatherings on Tuesday brought the virus to our event on Thursday. It ended up being a super-spreader event. I don't know how many people were infected that night, because most senators did not share that private data with the caucus. But after the event, at least four of us tested positive for COVID-19. I was one of them, and so was Jerry Relph.

Maralee and I traveled to Fort Myers, Florida, the next day, and we did not know we had COVID until we were at our hotel on Fort Myers Beach. It turned out to be a very mild case, and we needed to quarantine on the beach for almost two weeks. Had I not received a call from others that had tested positive for COVID, I doubt I would have even tested, because my symptoms were so mild. It turned out to be very relaxing quarantine; I was forced to stay on the beach for two weeks.

But Jerry Relph's case was not mild. Tragically Jerry died from COVID, and I was devastated. He was a good friend and senator. If only he had not come to the party. One thing about Jerry was that he attended everything. He jumped with both feet into politics and refused to take a back seat on anything. Even though at the age of seventy-six it might have been wise for him not to attend, he came anyway.

I was accused by some Democrats and one of his relatives of being responsible for his death. His wife, Peggy, who was also at the event, was very gracious to me and did not blame me.

Regardless, I lost a good friend. COVID was real, and folks who were older and/or had certain morbidities were definitely at risk of death.

We kept the information about the event private at first, and in hindsight, the Democrats should have been notified immediately. We were not in session, which meant that there was not a lot of activity around the Senate building anyway. Regardless, our Senate GOP staff members were encouraged to stay home until we knew more. In the end no one was infected beyond the event, including nonpartisan staff and Democratic staff.

Trump's Prediction That He Will Get Vaccines Out by December 2020 Is True

We needed the vaccines, and as they were ready to go, the focus was on getting the vaccines produced and out to those that wanted them.

By December of 2020 the vaccines started rolling out, as promised by Trump. It took a while for the vaccines to be produced and offered to everyone. Once seniors were vaccinated, the number of deaths started to decline. Some said that the vaccines were more dangerous than COVID-19, but the data I saw would contradict that position. The vaccines had some side effects, and the government apparently hid some of those from the public. But purely empirical numbers showed that deaths and hospital stays by various age groups for those vaccinated were about a third compared to the groups that were not.

Because kids were never at serious risk of death from COVID, I personally would not have encouraged children to be vaccinated. But even then, it should have been a parental decision, and after age 18, a decision for the individual to make. I was never worried about getting the virus, which I did. I was never worried about getting vaccinated either, and I did. We had a government trip planned out of the country, and the only way we could go at the time was to get vaccinated. It was an easy choice for me. I wanted to travel, and getting the vaccine was the only way to do so. However, for some, especially in Minnesota under Governor Waz, the decision was more difficult. Some were required to get vaccinated to continue to attend college or keep their jobs. It should have always been a choice, but it wasn't, and that was wrong.

GOVERNOR WALZ WON'T GIVE UP EMERGENCY POWERS

As the vaccines were produced and distributed, COVID began to lose its grip on the world. But as 2021 dragged on, even though there was no reasonable case that could be made to justify our governor continuing to keep emergency powers, he kept them.

The final lever to be used to get rid of his powers had to wait till end of session. The pressure was mounting from many on my side of the aisle, but all I could do was take the heat and wait for the moment at the end of the session in mid-May.

COVID LESSONS LEARNED

There are many lessons that must be learned from the worst pandemic in our lifetime. The virus was real; the vaccines helped many and hurt some. And there are some things that we should never allow again, and those should be mentioned here. Lockdowns didn't work, keeping kids out of schools did more harm than good, and forcing people to wear a mask or take a vaccine was too much control by Governor Walz and other governors. The government must not manipulate the facts to fit their narrative. In the end the people will not trust anything that the government says when they do that. Finally, no governor should be able to use a pandemic for more than a year to run a state through emergency powers. Governor Walz and others were guilty of hanging on to the powers too long because of a perceived greater good. In the end though, that is a slippery slope we should not allow.

CHAPTER 18

TWO DEMOCRATIC SENATORS DEFECT

OVER MY YEARS as leader, I tried to recruit a few Democratic senators to switch to our side of the aisle. I came close more than once. These were always very secretive meetings, with just a few people on my side knowing what I was trying to do.

Democratic Senator Dan Sparks was from a rural southern Minnesota district. Each election cycle, the numbers were trending more and more toward the Republican side in his district. On most issues Sparks voted more like a Republican, and yet he was a Democratic senator. Just a few years earlier, we had similar conversations with Senator Lyle Koenen from Willmar, and Sparks remembered his outcome—he was not reelected.

I had tried several times to recruit Sparks. He was frustrated with the direction his caucus was going. Senators Jeremy Miller and Julie Rosen also were involved in trying to get him to switch over. We did the dance for months. Finally I said to him that if he did not switch, we would take him out, but that was not quite enough to move him over. That's exactly what happened in November of 2020, when Gene Dornink unseated him. Gene had come within ten points of defeating Sparks in the previous election, and this time, there was no stopping Gene Dornink. Later, Sparks said that he appreciated that I at least gave him the opportunity to switch before we crushed him.

In the 2020 election, Tom Bakk and David Tomassoni, both from the Iron Range in northeast Minnesota, won as Democrats, but their districts were also trending Republican. They saw many rural districts once controlled by Democrats were now served by Republican senators. But for them, more importantly, their party and governor no longer valued them. In addition, Republicans kept the majority in the Senate, and they would have little influence in the minority.

Republican Senator John Jasinski had built a very strong friendship with Senator Tomassoni, and I asked him to work on Tomassoni. Jasinski's friendship was genuine, and our offer to fully make him a part of our GOP team was real. Tomassoni was already well liked by most of our team.

Senator Tom Bakk and I had become friends, and we had a very good working relationship. I decided to approach him about switching over. It had happened before, but asking a former Senate majority leader to switch parties is a big deal.

SENATOR KENT REMOVES SENATOR BAKK AS DEMOCRATIC LEADER

In January of 2020, about a year earlier, Democrat Susan Kent challenged Tom Bakk for minority leadership. Tom was literally out of the country and got a call notifying him that at the upcoming Senate Democrats meeting, he was going to be removed from power.

He hung up the phone and canceled their upcoming meeting. About a month later, their epic battle came to a head, and I was told that Bakk lost control of his minority leadership role by one vote.

The old saying goes, if you are going to shoot the bear, you better make sure you kill it.

Obviously Senator Bakk was not happy. But neither was Senator Tomassoni. Most of the moderates were no longer in the Senate

Democrat caucus, and the few that were left were now outliers. Their Democratic governor, Walz, gave them little support for the needs of northeast Minnesota.

In addition I naturally connected more to Bakk and Tomassoni because we were all from the Iron Range. I worked in the mines and shared many similar political views. In fact, just before Tomassoni became a legislator, my dad had tried to hire him to become an insurance agent on the Iron Range.

Over my first four years as leader, I went out of my way to promote Iron Range projects. I wanted to help that area, but I also hoped that one day, we would either elect Republicans in that area or Bakk and Tomassoni would join us.

We kept the majority in the Senate, and now was the time to make the play. They now fit better with us. I called Senator Bakk up first because I knew if it was going to happen, he had to be on board first. And he was on board—for the right deal. When Bakk was on board, Tomassoni now had cover join us by forming a new alliance.

THE DEAL

The deal I made was that Bakk would become the Bonding chair and Tomassoni would become Higher Education chair. In addition, for a brief time, Tomassoni would become the president of the Senate. Finally, Bakk and Tomassoni would share a suite on the third floor of the Capitol, directly above the Senate majority leader's suite of offices. The Bakkasoni Suite, as they dubbed it, remained a fairly neutral place where members from both parties would stop in for refreshments and lively conversation.

The secret deal had been struck, but very few Republican senators knew what I was up to. Now I had to convince our team that allowing two Democrat senators to defect to our side and have prominent positions in our caucus was a good idea.

At first there was some opposition, especially when I didn't demand that they publicly declare that they would be Republicans.

I knew they had new challenges in their local districts because of this decision, and I wasn't going to require that declaration yet. But as the reality of this new alignment sunk in, everyone could see that it was worth the risk. We knew there was some risk, but the possible rewards far outweighed it.

Making promises to Bakk and Tomassoni meant that a couple of Republican senators would have to give up committees they chaired. Senator Senjem was willing to give up his Bonding chair, but he would only do it if he got to oversee Energy. This was tricky on two fronts. First the chair of that committee would have to step aside. Next Senjem pushed for more aggressive green energy policies than the caucus majority preferred. That was up to me to watch. To safeguard the caucus position, I stacked the committee with more energy conservative members. For an energy policy to pass, it would require consensus from a diverse group of GOP legislators.

Senator Jeremy Miller gave up the Higher Education chair to Tomassoni and agreed that Tomassoni could briefly be president of the Senate.

In the end, once those assignments were completed, they transitioned easily into our caucus, and their input in our meetings was well received. By the end of the first year, Bakk fit in so well that he was seriously considered for majority leader again after me—as a Republican. Senator Miller prevailed as the next majority leader, but a number of Republican senators thought Bakk could have been the next leader.

A First: Two Defectors Switch at the Same Time

There was never a time that I am aware of in Minnesota politics when two Democratic senators defected at the same time; it was a real coup. The timing for the defection was perfect. Senator Susan Kent was demanding I step down as Senate leader because I was responsible for a COVID super-spreader event, where Jerry Relph was infected with COVID, causing his eventual death.

In addition, with our new one-seat majority, I had a Republican senator trying to make a power play against me. He was not trying to take my position, but he was using the one-vote majority to make certain demands.

Little did either of these people know that I had just cut a deal with two Democratic senators to align with the Republican Senate. Now we would function as 36–31, which made passing bills out of the Senate much easier. No one senator could try to make a power play against me anymore.

As part of the deal, I did not demand that they publicly become Republicans, but I did demand that they align with us on all procedural votes, which allowed me to govern much more easily.

Both Bakk and Tomassoni now caucused with the Republicans. Their input was welcomed and really no different than the few other moderate Republican senators on our team. But they brought a wealth of perspective as to what the Senate Democrats might be thinking and why they might be passionate about something we were not passionate about.

In the end Tomassoni was at heart still a Democrat from the Iron Range. Bakk became an alternate Republican state delegate from the Iron Range that year. But both were really still old-time Democrats. Bakk would often say, "I did not leave the Democratic Party; the Party left me." And that party was now run by Tim Walz.

CHAPTER 19

EMERGENCY POWERS TAKEN FROM GOVERNOR WALZ

T HE TWO-YEAR BUDGET of 2021 was difficult to manage because most of the legislative meetings were usually done via Zoom. Negotiations with the governor were also usually done this way. Face-to-face meetings for this kind of negotiation are far better, and I think you get a better product as well, but that is not what we were doing.

THE FINAL LEVER TO END EMERGENCY POWERS

As we were closing in on ending the session, the biggest demand I had was that before we agreed to pass the final budget for state government finance, emergency powers must end. This was the final lever I had to pull. The budget is usually divided into about eight separate bills funding K–12 education, higher education, health and human services, the department of natural resources, transportation, and the like. The one piece of the budget I would hold up funding for was the executive branch and the legislative branch. This was the state government finance bill. I didn't want to hold up the rest of the budgets, which directly impact the people of Minnesota, but I was willing to hold up the state government budget.

Speaker Hortman knew I was serious about this demand. When I said something, I meant it. Where the 2019 budget had many discussions between me and the governor, in 2021, I had most of my discussions with Speaker Hortman. I did this for a couple of reasons. The governor was now in the groove and much stronger in his role as governor, especially because he was still operating under emergency powers. The second reason was that Speaker Hortman was now also stronger as a legislative leader, and some of the decisions I wanted to make were best discussed with her to find a compromise.

THE TRADE

Speaker Hortman, like former Senate Majority Leader Bakk years before, wanted a major upgrade to her legislative building. I wanted emergency powers to end. This was a trade I was willing to make. I felt like ending emergency powers was very important to Minnesota. I also felt the pressure from the Republican base, who were increasingly upset that I could not remove the governor's emergency powers.

PRESSURE TO SHUT DOWN THE GOVERNMENT

They did not understand that I did not have the power to remove his emergency powers without the help of the Democrat-controlled House. Outside influencers were suggesting that we shut down the government until emergency powers ended. They didn't care who it hurt; they just wanted it done. They did not realize that in the 2017 shutdown, our supreme court clarified that the courts do not have the authority to keep parts of government open and other parts closed. It would all be closed down in future shutdowns. That would be a disaster for everyone. The highway patrol would not be funded, nursing homes would not be funded, permits would not be issued, and the list goes on. I did not want that to happen, and at the same time, emergency powers needed to end.

The House Democrats needed a big enough carrot to go against their own governor, and they needed legislative permission from the Senate to fix the mold and safety concerns of their building. That was the carrot. I don't believe they would have ever supported taking away the governor's emergency powers for any trade if they didn't think he needed to give up the powers.

The language Speaker Hortman and I verbally agreed to was that the House could do a study for what would be required to address the needs of the State Office Building, which included safety measures and addressing a mold issue. In addition, funding would be provided for the cost of those improvements. It was a good trade, but that agreement changed after Democrats took control of the Senate, giving Democrats the trifecta, or complete control. When that happened, the State Office Building improvement plan was dramatically expanded, allowing the building to expand beyond its present footprint. It was going to cost a lot more. What they decided to do after was a more ambitious design.

I had also tried to get rid of the fines assessed to small businesses during the lockdowns. I tried to trade giving the governor a raise for an agreement to waive any fines assessed to businesses that violated the closure of their businesses during COVID. That one failed.

As we headed to the finish line, many budget bills passed, but then the state government finance bill was up. This is the one that funds the executive branch and the legislative branch, and it was up and ready to pass. The problem was it did not have the exact language I had asked for to immediately end the governor's emergency powers. Instead, the language was vaguer and said the powers ended a little later. That was not the deal; it was not clear cut. I immediately recessed the Senate. I would not pass that bill without the ending of emergency powers at the same time. That was my vocal public promise.

Governor Walz did not want to give up his power. As he saw that Hortman and I were going to end them, to save face, he started to publicly say he was leading that charge to gradually give them up. First, he said he would give them up a month or so down the road. Then as he saw the language, that it was really going to happen, he tried to say he was cooperating, but he was not.

In recess, Hortman asked me what the holdup was. I said it is not the deal we agreed to, and I would not pass the state government finance bill without the emergency powers ending. She asked if I would come over to her suite next to the House chamber. I agreed, and I walked over with my chief of staff, Craig Sondag. Once we got there, I went into the room alone with Hortman. It was always nice to walk into meetings with a few trusted advisors, but often the deal is made alone.

TIM WALZ'S EMERGENCY POWERS ENDED AGAINST HIS WILL

In the end Hortman agreed to end the powers immediately, against the governor's wishes. She in turn was going to get her building remodeled. The governor made the best of it, but it was way past time for his powers to end.

That two-year budget felt like a draw. We couldn't agree on everything and left a lot of the surplus on the bottom line for the following year. I did not want to spend it, and the Democrats did not want more tax relief, so it was held over for discussion about what to do with the surplus in the following year.

We finished the session, and COVID gradually became a distant memory.

But looking back, some decisions were clearly better than others. Polling in the Twin Cities at the time showed that a majority of Minnesota's supported the governor's more extreme positions, like lockdowns and forced masks. I think perhaps the polls were favorable because the citizens of each state were rooting for their governors to be successful against COVID-19. In the end, I'm simply glad the pandemic is behind us, and the emergency powers were finally taken from Governor Tim Walz.

CHAPTER 20

WALZ PROVIDED POOR OVERSIGHT OF TAXPAYERS' MONEY

A s COVID AND Walz's emergency powers were in the rear-view mirror, another ugly problem began to come into focus, and that was Governor Walz's oversight of his agencies.

The governor is responsible for properly administering and dispersing the tax dollars that come into the state. Normally, nothing newsworthy comes of this responsibility, but in Minnesota, under Walz's leadership, multiple problems came to light.

News broke that an organization called Feeding Our Future was under investigation for misusing State of Minnesota funds that were funneled to them through the Minnesota Department of Education. In addition to law enforcement, the nonpartisan Office of the Legislative Auditor (OLA) delved into this accusation, as well as others.

The waste and fraud that has been allowed under Governor Tim Walz's administration has been astronomical.

Governor Walz had been governor for almost four years when problem programs started surfacing. The OLA, in testimony, said that his administration was not taking the OLA recommendations seriously.[1]

The Minnesota Department of Education's inadequate oversight allowed Feeding Our Future to steal $250 million. When confronted, Education Commissioner Willie Jet refused to take responsibility and instead blamed the fraudsters.

In a newly surfacing debacle, oversight of the frontline worker pay program, which gave a small bonus to folks who were working on the frontlines during the COVID-19 pandemic, came into question. As it turns out, the Department of Labor and Industry, who gave oversight to that program, paid out over $500 million in funds from the program to ineligible people.

And now it looks like Medicaid fraud may be next.

OLA Auditor Judy Randall said she noticed Walz's agencies becoming less receptive to audits that criticize their work.[2]

With agency after agency, under Governor Tim Walz there has been terrible oversight, responsible for record amounts of waste and fraud. Governor Walz's agencies lack a regulatory mindset, which means the likelihood of more fraud and waste will only go up.

If this is how Governor Walz provided oversight in Minnesota, how would he be any different as vice president of the United States?

CHAPTER 21

WALZ WITH THE TRIFECTA IN MINNESOTA

I MADE A DECISION to run for governor against Walz in 2022 but was not endorsed as the GOP candidate in Minnesota in May of 2022. I promised that if I were not endorsed, I would not run to the primary, and I kept that promise.

My time had come to an end in the Minnesota Senate, and I did not seek reelection. I moved back up to central Minnesota and started running my insurance agency again. It was a lot easier.

In the November 2022 election Walz handily won reelection as governor, and Democrats took complete control of the House and Senate. Governor Walz had a trifecta. The prior year, Governor Walz and the Republican Senate could not agree with what to do with a surplus that ended up growing to $18 billion.

There was a tentative agreement to spend one-third, give tax relief with one-third, and leave the rest on the bottom line, unspent. I supported that position, but it did not get done.

But with the November election of 2022 and Walz having complete control, Governor Walz spent *all* of the $18 billion surplus and added a number of new programs. In addition to spending the surplus and increasing the Minnesota state budget nearly 40 percent in 2023, he *raised* taxes.[1]

Tim Walz Spent Minnesota into a Future Deficit

As I write this book, the future budget projections in Minnesota show a future budget *shortfall*, or structural deficit, of billions of dollars again. If Walz did that to Minnesota's budget, what could he do to our federal budget?

Governor Walz started his political career as a congressman from District One in southeast Minnesota. He wore an NRA hat and touted pro-gun support. But as he made a decision to run for governor in 2018, he no longer touted his pro-gun record and went the opposite direction. Now he was pandering to the metro area and changed his tune.

He started out as governor in divided government and initially showed promise as a pragmatic moderate. That changed as soon as he had the opportunity to drive his true agenda, a very liberal, progressive agenda.

But his leadership has not led to better results. Math and reading scores for Minnesota students have dropped since Walz became governor.[2] Minnesota's ranking of best places for businesses also is continuing to drop.[3] Once he had the trifecta, taxes went up, and Minnesotans earning more than $200,000 a year are leaving moving out of the state.[4] Under his dominance, Minnesota is trending in the wrong direction.

Minnesota's positions based on compromises between Democrats and Republicans over the last few decades were swept aside.

For example, Walz champions abortion rights like there's a trophy to be given out for having one. Gone are the days of Democrats saying they support abortion because it needed to be "safe and rare." Walz pushed extreme abortion legislation that defunded organizations that helped pregnant women who wanted to keep their babies. Gone are the laws that notified the parents if their fifteen-year-old daughter was pregnant. Any common-sense compromises related to abortions laws were swept aside.

Small businesses were already struggling under high taxes, but in 2023, Walz made it worse by passing an oppressive paid family leave mandate. The mandate will tax every employee and employer in the state. In addition, up to twenty weeks of leave is potentially available *every year*, even if the small business has only *one* employee. It is not workable, but they passed the law anyway.

Another burdensome program passed in 2023 requires utility companies to procure 100 percent of the energy they serve to customers to be carbon-free or renewable sources by 2040. In concept this sounds wonderful; in practice it likely won't work during bitter cold days in Minnesota. Then what will they do?

Before 2023, school kids who could not afford a lunch were provided one for free. Tim Walz passed legislation that provides free breakfast and lunch to every student every day. But it really isn't free; the taxpayers have to pay for that.

It didn't surprise me that all these programs were rammed through. I knew what Walz would do if he had the chance. And it's that same kind of attitude that he would bring to the White House if he became the vice president. He campaigned for governor with the slogan "One Minnesota," but he is not a consensus builder. He wipes out any ideas but his own. His country charm is deceptive because he does not represent rural American values.

CHAPTER 22

CONTRAST MY EXPERIENCE WITH TRUMP

W HEN I CONTEMPLATED whether to write a chapter about Trump, I felt it was worthwhile to contrast my experiences with Trump and Walz.

I have no idea when Trump decided to run for president. Prophets and pundits had proclaimed and pondered the idea for decades. But by 2015 the Trump machine was moving forward with momentum.

At first, with more than a dozen contenders for the GOP nomination, I thought there was no way that Trump would be the nominee. He was at best a wild card. He wasn't even close in my mind as to who would be the best candidate the first time around.

As the months rolled by, he somehow managed to stay in the lead. One by one, his Republican opponents began to drop out. At the same time, those that loved Trump became more and more excited and vocal about their support for him. He was a phenomenon. No one running at this level had ever been anything like him. He had bold positions. He was abrasive to his Republican adversaries, and yet he kept building momentum.

Once he became the endorsed candidate, the real mudslinging started. Democrats, with Hillary Clinton leading the charge, were sure they would demolish Trump. But just like many of his Republican adversaries, he vanquished "crooked Hillary." Outrageous name calling became part of his persona. His "you punch me, I demolish you" approach ended up garnering support from unlikely groups. Nationally, many blue-collar workers got behind him. More minorities than usual also supported him. He wanted to drain the swamp, and he meant it.

He promised many things: tax cuts, conservative judges, more blue-collar jobs, stronger military with an expectation of more responsibility from our allies, protecting life and the second amendment, and more.

President Trump Keeps His Word Regarding Campaign Promises

I remember one of my own final debates against my Democratic opponent for state senate. The question was asked, "Do you support Trump?" It was meant as a negative. How could anyone support Trump?

My answer was firm: "Yes, I support Trump. At least he says he is pro-life, and at least he says he supports the second amendment, etc." I really didn't know at the time if he would follow through with his campaign promises. His track record on these issues was not inspiring. But in the end, as president, he followed through with more of his campaign promises than any other president I could remember.

The only top-tier promise he did not get done was the promise to get rid of Obamacare. Even this one he tried to do, but Republican Senator John McCain stopped him. In this case Trump's early inexperience and conflicts with McCain, a more moderate Republican senator, cost him McCain's support. That one vote buried Trump's chances of repealing Obamacare.

It is true he did not finish the southern border wall, and he did not completely eliminate illegal immigration, but that was no fault of his own. Even without the help of Congress, Trump dramatically reduced illegal immigration and built over five hundred miles of border walls, despite Democratic opposition.

Part of Trump's success was that he surrounded himself with good leaders. In addition, if one of his appointees did not measure up to his expectations, he was quick to remove them.

IN THE BEAST WITH TRUMP

I met President Trump for the first time when he came to Duluth, Minnesota, in June of 2018. As leader of the Senate, I was asked to meet him on the Duluth airport tarmac. Anytime you get to meet the president, it's a big deal, and I was excited to meet him.

By this time, he had proven that he was going to be a good president for our country. He was a decisive leader. He did what he said he was going to do. He took risks if he thought they would help America.

Only three Republicans leaders were invited to meet him: Lieutenant Governor Fischbach, congressional candidate Pete Stauber, and me. As we talked, I had the opportunity to offer him my challenge coin, a coin with a Roman soldier on one side and Ephesians 6:10–11 on the other side of the coin: "Be strong in the Lord and in the power of His might. Put on the whole armor of God."

Usually the Secret Service forbids any tokens or gifts to be given to the President, but in a small group setting, exceptions are often made. President Trump graciously accepted my challenge coin and then asked if I wanted to go with him for a ride.

I was not expecting to ride in "the beast," as his transportation is affectionately called, but I said yes right away. Candidate Stauber also said yes. We jumped into the back of his limousine and started heading to a forum on taconite mining in northeast Minnesota. I was planning on heading to the civic center for the upcoming rally, so I was wondering how I was going to get there when the forum ended.

The ride was about twenty minutes. President Trump peppered

us with questions. He wanted to know if his policies were helping in Minnesota. I was able to affirm that his position on foreign steel was helping the taconite industry in Minnesota. I affirmed that I liked that he was focusing on the campaign promises he made. We talked about the southern border and his position that children should not be separated from their parents at the border. That did not mean that President Trump wanted to let them into the country illegally, but he also did not think it was a good idea to separate families. I think it was that day that he signed an executive order preventing that from happening.

Trump also talked about North Korea in the car ride and finding solutions to that thorny issue. It was just a week or so after our ride that President Trump visited Kim Jong Un, the North Korean leader, on North Korean soil.

I found out later that sometime earlier, President Trump had secretly sent CIA Director Mike Pompeo to North Korea to pave the way for a possible visit from the president of the United States. No sitting president had ever visited North Korea, but President Trump was taking a bold risk to try to find a way to relaunch stalled nuclear talks. Secretary of State Rex Tillerson should have been the one brokering the visit, but, if he didn't know it yet, he probably knew then that he was on his way out of the Trump administration.

TRUMP DEEPLY CARES ABOUT AMERICA

These issues and more were discussed in that first twenty-minute car ride. I felt so at ease with the president that I honestly told him that he was not my first choice for president. He asked me who I supported, and when I mentioned the name, he told me that that person would have never won—he was probably right. I was left with a few impressions as a result of that ride. Trump cared deeply about America and admired the common folk of our land. As we would drive by hordes of enthusiastic supporters, President Trump would often say, "Look at all the great people." He was not condescending; he was one of them.

We arrived at the mining forum, an event I was not scheduled to be at, and President Trump asked the organizers to add a front row chair for me to sit in. As the forum was about to end, it occurred to me that I did not have a ride to the main event at the civic center. When a president comes to an event, the Secret Service scours the location ahead of time for any hint of danger to the president. Then they lock the place down at least an hour before the president arrives. No one gets in after it's locked down. So how was I going to get in?

A SECOND RIDE WITH THE PRESIDENT

I decided that the only way I was going to get into the civic center was if I asked the president for another ride in the beast. When the forum ended, President Trump could either exit to the left or right. If he exited to the right, he would pass within about twenty feet of me. If he exited left, my day was done, and I would not be at the civic center. President Trump exited right, going by me. The Secret Service was already creating a greater separation between me and the president. I raised my voice and say, "Mr. President!" Trump turned to me and waited for my question. "Do you mind if I catch another ride with you to the civic center?" I asked. He motioned for me to join him, and off we went to the civic center. It all seemed surreal, but it was a tremendous privilege that I will never forget.

Candidate Stauber was also with us again and was a bit star struck during the ride, but he was bold enough to ask the president if he could have a selfie with him. Well, if he was going to do it, so was I. We were switching seats in the back of the limo to get the best photos, and the president was game enough to let us do it. It was just me and Pete Stauber with the president. There was no chief of staff with us, just the two secret service agents in the front seat and a whole caravan of other support folks behind and in front of us.

It was likely that I would not have a moment like this again, so I'm really glad I got a photo of the event. Pete Stauber ended up becoming a congressman and has been a fierce advocate for northeast Minnesota.

In my photo with Trump, we are both smiling inside the beast. Some of my friends asked if it really happened, as it looked photoshopped. Others were upset that I was smiling with the president. I told them that I have photos smiling with two different Democratic governors too. One way or the other, some will be upset that I'm smiling in my photos.

Another brief visit with the president that stands out was when he came to Minnesota on September 30, 2020.

We were in the middle of COVID and an election year. While Biden was hunkered down in someplace safe, Trump was fearlessly traveling the country to promote his presidential accomplishments. Trump landed in Minneapolis, and Maralee and I were the first to meet him as he came off of Air Force One. To meet the president or vice president, a COVID test was required to make sure we were not infected. The White House didn't want our leaders getting COVID, if possible. At the time, a six-foot distance was also recommended between any two people. We tried to keep that distance between us and the president.

The meeting was the day after his first debate with Biden. The night before, I was watching the debate with Trump supporters in Little Falls, while Maralee was watching the debate at home.

As we chatted with President Trump on the MSP tarmac, he asked me if I thought he was going to win Minnesota, because Reagan lost to Mondale here. I said to him that I thought he would win Minnesota; he was within two points in the first election. Both Maralee and I enjoyed the conversation.

We then asked the president if we could get a photo with him, and we stood shoulder to shoulder—not the COVID recommendation of six feet apart—for some great photos. Little did we know that the president had COVID at that meeting.

PRESIDENT TRUMP HAS COVID-19— DID HE INFECT US?

It was determined soon after we met the president that Hope Hicks, one of Trump's key advisors, had come down with COVID. Then, President Trump was tested, and he was also infected with the virus.[1]

We all watched as Trump navigated through his own experience with COVID. He faced it bravely, and in the end, he navigated through the illness very well. Because we had been in direct contact with the president, we had to quarantine for two weeks. We didn't end up getting it, and though I know COVID was serious, I joked that if I was going to get it, I wished I had got it from the president of the United States.

CAPITOL INVITES

I was invited to other events at the Capitol with Trump, including one of his Christmas parties after he lost the election. But one of the more special events I attended was the Abraham Accords at the White House. I think every president in my lifetime, as far back as I can remember, has sought to bring more peace to the Middle East, but few have accomplished much. The Abraham Accords were a series of agreements to normalize relationships between Israel and several Arab states. They were signed in the second half of 2020, but there was a press conference with Trump and Netanyahu, as well as a gathering at the White House, to announce Trump's Middle East peace plan, which the accords were part of, on January 28, 2020.

ATTENDING THE ABRAHAM ACCORDS

Only about 150 people were invited to the event, squeezed into the East Room of the White House. My invite came through Minnesota State Senator Jeremy Miller, the president of the Senate at that time. Jeremy is Jewish and was asked by the White House if he would like to attend the meeting. He could bring one guest with him if he decided to go. Jeremy was undecided about going when he asked me if I had any interest. I told Jeremy that this event was very significant, and I would love to attend with him. We had to go and did.

It was a who's who of supporters of Israel, and we were privileged to be a part of that gathering.

TRUMP SHOULD HAVE RECEIVED THE NOBEL PEACE PRIZE

People have been trying to find a way to bring more peace to the Middle East forever, but Trump was actually doing it. It was the first actual Middle East peace deal in over twenty-five years, and the leaders involved should have received the Nobel Peace Prize— but they didn't.[2] As the meeting began, Prime Minister of Israel Benjamin Netanyahu and President Trump strolled up the aisle together to the podium. Together they announced the goals of the peace plan. Netanyahu was grateful for many good leaders, from both parties. But he was particularly impressed with the work that Trump was doing to support Israel and peace in the Middle East.

THE MIDDLE EAST IS BACK IN CHAOS WHEN BIDEN IS PRESIDENT

As has happened many times before, since Trump left office as president, the Middle East is far from peace again. The rise of anti-Semitism is greater than I ever recall in my lifetime. Hamas has been emboldened and struck Israel a wicked blow on October 7, 2023. They brutally murdered many women and children in a surprise terrorist attack. As I'm writing this, Israel is pushing back, trying to drive Hamas out of Gaza. The idea of a two-state solution—Israel and Palestinians in Gaza—seemed possible in the past. But if most Palestinians want to destroy Israel, a two-state solution is out of the question. If Hamas and those that hate Israel stop shooting, there can be peace. If Israel stops defending themselves, they cease to exist.

It was a privilege to meet the president and vice president a number of times, both in Minnesota and in Washington, DC. It never got old. I can see how people get caught up in the trappings of power. For me, I just genuinely felt honored to rub shoulders with people of influence. My hope was always that I would provide a meaningful thought to the conversation that would help them become better leaders.

I thought that Trump's political career was over after the election of 2020, but somehow, Trump came roaring back. Nefarious Democratic operatives at many levels have done everything they can to stop his rise again, but I don't think anything will stop him from being president again.

It appeared to be a redo of the prior 2020 election between Trump and Biden, but then the infamous debate happened; President Biden flopped, and Trump crushed him.

President Biden performed poorly as our leader, and enough people that supported Biden over Trump the first time now realize that President Biden was not who they hoped he would be. But the last straw for many tentative Biden supporters was his obvious cognitive decline. The live debate could not hide Biden's actual cognitive ability.

President Biden's "friends" were now his political enemies. He had to go; there was no way he could beat Trump. The drumbeat to remove him got louder and louder. Something had to give.

TRUMP BEATS THE ABUSIVE USE OF COURTS AGAINST HIM

The Democrats used the courts to try to stop Donald Trump, and they failed. At first, they thought they had got him, when former President Trump was convicted of felonies in a New York court.[3] But then, in another court case, the US Supreme Court ruled that all prior presidents, including Trump, were given substantial presidential immunity for public acts during their presidencies.[4]

Trump prevailed against the misuse of the courts to stop him.

Trump Miraculously Survives an Attempted Assassination

Then on Saturday, July 13, 2024, Trump miraculously survived an assassination attempt at a rally in Pennsylvania. Twenty-year-old would-be assassin Matthew Crooks only nicked Trump's ear when shooting at his head from just 130 yards away. It is a miracle Trump was not killed or seriously injured. One innocent bystander was tragically killed in the incident. Trump was hit and ducked to the ground, but he rose defiant and triumphant. You never really know how a person will respond when faced with death. In Trump's case, he faced fear and death head on. That is a character quality I want in our leaders. Caving to fear is debilitating. Facing fear is inspiring.

The speed at which political landscape shifts and Trump's ability to navigate each obstacle in his path only solidified my conviction that Trump will return to the Oval Office. If that comes to pass, my hope is that he will help to unify our country this time as president. His first term as president was clearly as a general, and he did get us back on track. Will his second term be more like an encouraging father? I hope so. Fathers don't coddle but are still loving. Fathers expect the best from us. Fathers help us grow up, toughen up, and stand up. Good fathers also expect strong character qualities.

Attempted Assassination of President Reagan

When President Reagan was wounded in an attempted assassination on March 30, 1981, and almost died, it changed him. His personal faith in God appeared to grow much stronger and more important after that. His friend Democratic Speaker Tip O'Neill was one of the first visitors to see Reagan in the hospital while he was recovering. Tip prayed the Twenty-Third Psalm over the president.[5]

The LORD is my shepherd, I shall not want. He makes me lie down in green pastures; He leads me besides quiet waters. He restores my soul; He guides me in the paths of righteousness for His name's sake. Even though I walk through the valley of the shadow of death, I fear no evil, for You are with me; Your rod and Your staff, they comfort me. You prepare a table before me in the presence of my enemies; You have anointed my head with oil; my cup overflows. Surely goodness and lovingkindness will follow me all the days of my life, and I will dwell in the house of the LORD forever.

—PSALM 23, NASB

Political adversaries, Ronald Reagan and Tip O'Neill together connected with the Almighty. Together they made America better. After the fight of this election season is over, we desperately need more of that. We must unite as a country.

But in what appears to be the final bend during the election of 2024, Biden was forced out and Kamala Harris became the Democrat nominee for president—without having to compete for the nomination.

The table has been set. President Trump will square off against Vice President Kamala Harris. Each has picked their running mate. Trump picked JD Vance. Harris picked Tim Walz.

WHOM WILL I VOTE FOR TO BE THE NEXT PRESIDENT AND WHY

For me, making my choice for who should be our next president is not about personality or flaws in the contenders; both candidates have flaws.

It's about leadership and the direction each candidate wants to take the country. Both presidential candidates have a record while serving at the White House. I'm making my decision based on what they have already done, not what they say they will do.

Past performance is the best indicator of future performance, in this case, as the next president of the United States. And in this election, I believe America is best served by a strong, decisive leader, and I believe that is Donald Trump.

It is a clear choice. Voting for Trump will make America safer and more prosperous. Voting for Harris and Walz embraces a path toward socialism and an America much different and weaker than what we were meant to be.

CHAPTER 23

BEHIND THE VEIL: PRIVATE CONVERSATIONS WITH GOVERNOR WALZ

TEXT STRINGS, PHONE CALLS, AND EMAILS WITH GOVERNOR TIM WALZ

MUCH OF WHAT I wrote about in this book about my interaction with Governor Tim Walz reflected the regular contact I had with Governor Walz and also his chief of staff, Chris Schmitter. I still have all the texts that we exchanged through the COVID pandemic. Those texts also captured the helpless feeling and deep frustration I had toward Tim Walz as I watched building after building burn to the ground during the riots after the death of George Floyd.

In the texts we both asked questions of each other. I also challenged a number of decisions the governor made related to the COVID-19 pandemic that proved to be incorrect or too extreme. I talked privately first, and then publicly, about things that I was not making progress on privately.

I expressed my deep frustration with the snail-paced decisions related to the activation of the Minnesota National Guard. When Minneapolis needed a decisive leader most, Governor Walz dithered, and Minneapolis burned. These were the most tense text moments between us.

I have been public about my frustration with Governor Walz during that time, and I was glad that I kept the text strings to remind myself of what actually took place at that time. You can't spin the facts, and I have them.

When Tim Walz was picked as Kamala Harris' vice presidential candidate running mate, I was doing interviews about Walz with many national media outlets. One of them asked me if I had texts saved between me and Walz. I said I did. He then suggested that I should make them public and release them because they would provide historical context. Even though I seriously thought about making public the complete text conversations I had with Governor Tim Walz, I decided that I would not print the actual text communications for a few reasons.

First, politicians from different parties often make use of backchannel communications. It is important that this happen, and we don't want all our discussions conducted in public debate. Public officials need to build trust as much as possible, to get results people want and deserve. That has always been a part of my philosophy of government; we look to build relationships, especially with those who have different perspectives than my own. Releasing private conversations could betray a kind of understanding that legislators and other political leaders need. There are times we must speak directly and candidly, and that is best done in private.

Second, private communications need context, or they can be unfairly used. We have all seen the danger of taking a statement out of context, and I don't want to do that.

So instead of making the texts public, I will share my sense of those many conversations, and the intense frustration of those times in the difficult days of 2020. Plain and simple, we needed the National Guard presence during the riots, and needed it immediately after the first sign of trouble. I went public in those early days, criticizing the delay in response, and made my concerns known to Tim Walz during and after the riots.

During the riots, mostly from Walz's chief of staff, there was a series of excuses and political concerns that we should not speak out and put the governor in a bad light.

Much of the discussion centered on the then president of the Police Officers Federation of Minneapolis, the police union for the City of Minneapolis. The president released a public statement criticizing Walz for his lack of response, and indecisiveness in the Minneapolis riot crisis.

In my opinion, the governor and his staff seemed more concerned with managing and controlling critical responses than actually addressing the problems. I expressed this and tried to get the parties to speak but kept reinforcing that my main concerns were not being heard or my comments were being misunderstood.

This was not a moment to play the blame game or fret over one's political reputation; it was a time where decisive action was desperately needed, but instead they dithered.

For three nights the violence grew, culminating in setting the Third Precinct police building on fire. My constant attempts to get action were met with more political excuses and reasons they couldn't seem to help—nonsense! The situation needed strong and clear leadership—exactly what Governor Tim Walz could not, or would not, give. I lived through his unresponsive and excuse-ridden style of governance. I struggled through those days while more than fifteen hundred buildings were vandalized or destroyed, with half a billion dollars worth of damages.

Many of the initial COVID-19 pandemic responses were no better, and those conversations would be chapters long.

I saw these crisis moments and how Governor Walz handled them firsthand, up front, from my position in government, and people in this nation need to know about it.

But in the end, as I said, there is a real benefit in keeping the actual private conversations private.

CONCLUSION

I HAVE NEVER SEEN politics in the United States like today. We are deeply divided, but does that mean we can't still be civil? Those who have been asked to lead must try harder to show respect and value to each other.

At the same time, we must speak up for what we believe. If it's a warning cry, we can't be silent.

The first half of the book really shows the benefit of civility in government and how that can produce positive results bridging political divides.

The second half of the book is primarily about my role with Governor Tim Walz and why I ended up standing against him.

Tim Walz is the vice presidential candidate for Kamala Harris. He is applying for the second-most important position in our country and is first in line for the top spot. My comments about his leadership are not positive because he was not a good leader in a crisis, and when he leads, it's in the wrong direction. I'm concerned with what kind of leader he would be for our country. I don't like the direction he took the state of Minnesota in, and I'm concerned about what direction he would take our country in with presidential candidate Kamala Harris.

I am the reference that says, "Don't pick Tim Walz!"

Minnesota had back-to-back epic challenges with the COVID-19 pandemic and the riots after the death of George Floyd, and he responded poorly to both. I don't think he meant harm; I think he was just afraid of making the wrong decision. So he dithered instead of choosing decisively what to do.

Contrast that to President Trump, who immediately decided on a course of action related to COVID-19 by shutting down travel from China and speeding up the development of a vaccine for the COVID virus by allowing simultaneous testing instead of the slower process of sequential testing. He promised vaccines would be available in December 2020 for those that wanted them, and he delivered on that promise.

In the COVID crisis, Trump acted decisively; Tim Walz did not.

When Minneapolis was under siege after the death of George Floyd, Trump made himself available to Tim Walz for action. Trump was decisive; Walz was not. Tim Walz blamed the mayor of Minneapolis for not asking him properly for help. He then quipped that the National Guard was just a bunch of nineteen-year-old cooks anyway. Instead of taking responsibility for this epic failure, he blamed others.

Walz comes from Nebraska, and after moving to Minnesota to become a teacher, he served as a rural Minnesota congressman. But in his first bid to be Minnesota's governor, he was caught on video describing rural Minnesota's election map as mostly rocks and cows, offending those who lived in rural Minnesota.[1]

He may have country charm, but he can't say he represents rural America when his policies and glib statements reflect the opposite. The majority of rural Minnesota did not support him as governor. In his successful reelection for governor in 2022, Walz got fewer votes in his former rural congressional district than the Republican challenger did.

On the world stage Trump as president kept us out of all wars and kept our borders from being overrun. Biden and Harris have done the opposite, taking very little decisive action.

Our country is navigating dangerous times in the world, and now is the time for a decisive and courageous leader like Trump and not people like Walz or Harris.

Like all elections, it feels as if it is the most important of my lifetime. I don't know what the results will be. Regardless, I will accept the results. Either way, as the Holy Scriptures command, I will pray for our leaders. They will need it.

"First of all, then, I urge that entreaties and prayers, petitions and thanksgivings, be made on behalf of all men, for kings and all who are in authority so that we may lead a tranquil and quiet life in all godliness and dignity. This is good and acceptable in the sight of God our Savior" (1 Tim. 2:1–3).

Choose wisely, America!

ENDNOTES

CHAPTER 1

1.   It took William Wilberforce over twenty years to abolish the slave trade in England. Slavery was completely abolished on August 1, 1834, about a year after Wilberforce's death.

2.   Sarah Pruitt, "5 Things You May Not Know About Abraham Lincoln, Slavery and Emancipation," History, updated June 23, 2020, https://www.history.com/news/5-things-you-may-not-know-about-lincoln-slavery-and-emancipation.

3.   Brian Kilmeade, *Teddy and Booker T.: How Two American Icons Blazed a Path for Racial Equality* (Sentinel, 2023), 116–117, https://www.amazon.com/Teddy-Booker-T-American-Equality/dp/0593543823. The entire book is worth reading. It describes a unique relationship between Booker T. Washington and Teddy Roosevelt.

4.   Michael Ray, "London Bombings of 2005," *Encyclopaedia Britannica*, updated June 30, 2024, https://www.britannica.com/event/London-bombings-of-2005 https://www.britannica.com/event/London-bombings-of-2005.

5.   "Racial and Religious Hatred Bill," UK Parliament, updated June 9, 2005, https://publications.parliament.uk/pa/cm200506/cmbills/011/2006011.htm; "Racial and Religious Hatred Act 2006," *The Guardian*, January 19, 2009, https://www.theguardian.com/commentisfree/libertycentral/2008/dec/16/racial-religious-hatred-act.

6.   Doug Grow, "Christian-based Teen Challenge Treatment Program Prompts Fight over State Funding," MinnPost, April 26, 2013, https://www.minnpost.com/politics-policy/2013/04/christian-based-teen-challenge-treatment-program-prompts-fight-over-state-fu/.

CHAPTER 2

1.   C.J., "State Lawmaker Dines with Porn Star," Minnesota Star Tribune, June 17, 2010, https://www.startribune.com/state-lawmaker-dines-with-porn-star/96586419.

CHAPTER 3

1.   Tom Scheck, " A $6 Billion Deficit and Already Little Agreement," MPR News, December 3, 2010, https://www.mprnews.org/story/2010/12/03/state-budget-deficit-6-2-billion-governor.

Chapter 4

1.   CBN, "Demos Shakarian with Harald Bredesen," CBN, accessed August 22, 2024, https://www.cbn.com/spirituallife/biblestudyandtheology/discipleship/shakarian0212.aspx?mobile=false&option=print.

Chapter 5

1.   "Truman Quotes," Truman Library Institute, accessed August 22, 2024, https://www.trumanlibraryinstitute.org/truman/truman-quotes/page/5/.

Chapter 13

1.   Author, text message to constituent, March 27, 2020.

Chapter 14

1.   Lucia Suarez Sand, "George Floyd Death: The Cities Where People Are Protesting and Rioting," Fox News, updated June 1, 2020, https://www.foxnews.com/us/george-floyd-death-here-are-the-cities-protesting.

2.   "Minneapolis Mayor Frey: 'Brick and mortar is not as important as life,'" KSTP, updated March 1, 2021, https://kstp.com/special-coverage/george-floyd/minneapolis-mayor-frey-brick-and-mortar-is-not-as-important-as-life/.

3.   Bob Kroll, text message to author, May 29, 2020.

4.   Jake Schneider, "KARE 11 Live Coverage of Minneapolis Riots - May 29, 2020: 'Explain to Us What the Plan Is,'" YouTube, June 25, 2020, https://www.youtube.com/watch?v=cCp-ItfIgNc.

5.   Susan Du, "Minneapolis Park Board Votes to Expel State Patrol from Shared Office Space," *Minnesota Star Tribune*, April 22, 2021, https://www.startribune.com/minneapolis-park-board-votes-to-expel-state-patrol-from-shared-cubicle/600048946.

6.   Frederick Melo, "Union Activists Boot MN National Guard from St. Paul Labor Center, Walz Says This Is 'Unacceptable,'" Pioneer Press, updated April 16, 2021, https://www.twincities.com/2021/04/15/to-shouts-of-dont-come-back-labor-activists-boot-minnesota-national-guard-from-st-paul-labor-center/.

7.   Chandelis Duster, "Waters Calls for Protesters to 'Get More Confrontational' If No Guilty Verdict Is Reached in Derek Chauvin Trial," CNN, updated April 19, 2021, https://www.cnn.com/2021/04/19/politics/maxine-waters-derek-chauvin-trial/index.html.

8.   "Senate Webcast – Thursday, July 9, 2020," Minnesota Senate, July 9, 2020, https://mnsenate.granicus.com/player/clip/5415?view_id=11&redirect=true.

9.   "Gov. Walz, Minneapolis Mayor Give Differing Accounts of Why National Guard Response to Unrest Was Delayed," CBS News, August 4, 2020, https://www.cbsnews.com/minnesota/news/gov-walz-minneapolis-mayor-give-differing-accounts-of-why-national-guard-response-to-unrest-was-delayed/.

10.   "Read Martin Luther King Jr.'s 'I Have a Dream' speech in its entirety," NPR, updated January 16, 2023, https://www.npr.org/2010/01/18/122701268/i-have-a-dream-speech-in-its-entirety.

CHAPTER 15

1.   PBS NewsHour, "WATCH LIVE: Minnesota Governor Tim Walz Holds News Conference," YouTube, June 10, 2020, https://www.youtube.com/watch?v=zVUUsdZXU30.

2.   Erin L. Thompson, "Meet the Indigenous Activist Who Toppled Minnesota's Christopher Columbus Statue," *Smithsonian*, February 3, 2022, https://www.smithsonianmag.com/history/meet-the-indigenous-activist-who-toppled-minnesotas-christopher-columbus-statue-180979488/; Kristi Belcamino, "Protesters Tear Down Christopher Columbus Statue on Minnesota Capitol Grounds," Pioneer Press, updated June 11, 2020, https://www.twincities.com/2020/06/10/protesters-tear-down-christopher-columbus-statue-on-minnesota-capitol-grounds/.

3.   Lt. Governor Peggy Flanagan, "All Minnesotans should feel welcome at the Minnesota State Capitol, and our state is long overdue for a hard look at the symbols, statues, and icons that were created without the input of many of our communities," X, June 10, 2020, 10:58 p.m., https://x.com/LtGovFlanagan/status/1270913187853066240.

4.   "Columbus and Sex Slavery," WallBuilders, May 29, 2023, https://wallbuilders.com/resource/columbus-and-sex-slavery/.

5.   Peter DeCarlo and Mattie Harper, "Minnesota, We Need to Talk About Our Columbus Monument," MinnPost, October 8, 2018, https://www.minnpost.com/politics-policy/2018/10/minnesota-we-need-to-talk-about-our-columbus-monument/.

6.   DeCarlo and Harper, "Minnesota, We Need to Talk About Our Columbus Monument."

CHAPTER 16

1.   Peter Callaghan, "'The Scope and Scale of This Is Stunning': Chronicling the First Year of COVID-19 Pandemic in Minnesota," MinnPost, March 5, 2021, https://www.minnpost.com/health/2021/03/the-scope-and-scale-of-this-is-stunning-one-year-of-the-covid-19-pandemic-in-minnesota/.

2. Cal Thomas, "Reagan and O'Neill: A More Civil Approach to Politics," Washington Times, April 12, 2023, https://www.washingtontimes.com/news/2023/apr/12/reagan-and-oneill-more-civil-approach-to-politics/.

3. Lesley Kennedy, "How Gorbachev and Reagan's Friendship Helped Thaw the Cold War," History, updated August 6, 2024, https://www.history.com/news/gorbachev-reagan-cold-war.

CHAPTER 20

1. Ryan Faircloth and Briana Bierschbach, "Many Millions Lost. Is the Walz Administration Taking Fraud and Waste Seriously Enough?," Minnesota Star Tribune, July 12, 2024, https://www.startribune.com/many-millions-lost-is-the-walz-administration-taking-fraud-and-waste-seriously-enough/600380214.

2. Faircloth and Bierschbach, "Many Millions Lost."

CHAPTER 21

1. Martha Njolomole, "Minnesota State Budget Is a Disaster Waiting to Happen, Thanks to Gov. Walz and DFL-Controlled Legislature," American Experiment, August 9, 2024, https://www.americanexperiment.org/minnesota-state-budget-is-a-disaster-waiting-to-happen-thanks-to-gov-walz-and-the-dfl-controlled-legislature/.

2. J. Patrick Coolican, "Walz Needs to Confront Test Scores in His Second Term," Minnesota Reformer, August 29, 2022, https://minnesotareformer.com/2022/08/29/walzs-biggest-failure-test-scores/.

3. John Phelan, "CEOs Agree with the Data: Minnesota Isn't a 'Top State for Business,'" American Experiment, May 1, 2024, https://www.americanexperiment.org/ceos-agree-with-the-data-minnesota-isnt-a-top-state-for-business/.

4. Peter Callaghan, "Are People Moving Out of Minnesota Because of High Taxes? Question Is 'an Easy One to Manipulate,'" MinnPost, December 14, 2023, https://www.minnpost.com/business/2023/12/are-people-moving-out-of-minnesota-because-of-high-taxes-question-is-an-easy-one-to-manipulate/.

CHAPTER 22

1. William Mansell, Emily Shapiro, and Meredith Deliso, "President Trump Taken to Walter Reed Medical Center," ABC News, October 3, 2020, https://abcnews.go.com/US/president-trump-lady-test-positive-covid-19/story?id=73380448.

2. Jackson Richman, "Why Didn't the Abraham Accords Win the Nobel Peace Prize?," Washington Examiner, October 13, 2021, https://www.washingtonexaminer.com/opinion/2589991/why-didnt-the-abraham-accords-win-the-nobel-peace-prize/.

3.   Chris Pandolfo, "What Happens After Trump's Conviction? Legal Experts Break It Down," Fox News, updated May 30, 2024, https://www.foxnews.com/politics/what-happens-trump-convicted-legal-experts-breakdown.

4.   Brooke Singman and Brianna Herlihy, "Trump Immunity Case; Supreme Court Rules Ex-Presidents Have Substantial Protection from Prosecution," Fox News, updated July 1, 2024, https://www.foxnews.com/politics/trump-immunity-case-supreme-court-rules-ex-presidents-substantial-protection-prosecution.

5.   Patrick Gavin, "Matthews Book: O'Neill, Reagan Bond," Politico, September 30, 2013, https://www.politico.com/story/2013/09/chris-matthews-book-tip-and-the-gipper-when-politics-worked-097585.

CONCLUSION

1.   "VIDEO: Tim Walz Attacks Rural Minnesota as 'Mostly Rocks and Cows,'" Republican Governors Association, November 2, 2017, https://www.rga.org/video-tim-walz-attacks-rural-minnesota-mostly-rocks-cows/.

ABOUT THE AUTHOR

Paul Gazelka is a small business owner in central Minnesota and author of the book *Marketplace Ministers*, which recounts his life story about integrating Christian faith into a person's workplace and community.

In 2004 he began his fourteen-year legislative career, often saying, "I wasn't looking for politics; politics found me." Through his legislative career, in a state that leans Democratic, he ended up serving as Minnesota's longest-serving Republican Senate majority leader in modern times.

Gazelka was Senate majority leader when vice presidential candidate Tim Walz was governor. Gazelka, who is diplomatically firm but kind, found himself standing against Tim Walz during the Minneapolis riots that occurred after the death of George Floyd in May 2020.

Gazelka's faith in Jesus played an important role in building bridges with the opposing side, in treating people the way he would want to be treated, and even in how he confronted Tim Walz when they disagreed.

Paul Gazelka can be reached at:

Email: paul@gazelka.com
Facebook: Senator Paul Gazelka
X: @paulgazelka

Made in the USA
Monee, IL
25 September 2024

66489855R00144